CATALOGUE OF MUSIC
IN THE
LIBRARY OF CHRIST CHURCH
OXFORD

CATALOGUE OF MUSIC
IN THE
LIBRARY OF CHRIST CHURCH
OXFORD

BY

G. E. P. ARKWRIGHT

WITH A PREFACE BY

T. B. STRONG

DEAN OF CHRIST CHURCH

PART I

WORKS OF ASCERTAINED AUTHORSHIP

Republished by S. R. Publishers Ltd 1971
First published by the Oxford University Press
1915

NOTE ON THE 1971 EDITION

Reprinted by courtesy of the Governing Body, Christ Church, Oxford.

An appendix has been included listing the manuscripts referred to in the text of the Catalogue, from which negative microfilms have been prepared and of which copies can now (1971) be supplied in microform.

The corrigenda which follow refer to errors in the text of the original edition.

CORRIGENDA

Page 10, line 1. *Beckwith*. Omit the name 'Christmas'.
Page 38, line 20. *Farinelli.* For 'Cristiano' *read* 'Giovanni'.
Page 71, line 28. *Leveridge. For* 'Calista' *read* 'Caligula'.
Page 86, line 6 from bottom. Insert reference number 945.
Page 124, Before line 8 from botton, insert WHYTE or WHITE (William).

© 1971
The Governing Body, Christ Church,
Oxford
ISBN O 85409 624 8

Reprinted in England by Kingprint Limited

CATALOGUE OF MUSIC

IN THE
LIBRARY OF CHRIST CHURCH
OXFORD

BY

G. E. P. ARKWRIGHT

WITH A PREFACE BY

T. B. STRONG

DEAN OF CHRIST CHURCH

PART I
WORKS OF ASCERTAINED AUTHORSHIP

HUMPHREY MILFORD
OXFORD UNIVERSITY PRESS
LONDON EDINBURGH GLASGOW NEW YORK
TORONTO MELBOURNE BOMBAY
1915

PREFACE

THE present volume, being Part I of the Catalogue of the Library of Music at Christ Church, contains a list of all the manuscript music of which the authorship is known; it is not a complete list of the whole Collection. There is besides the works catalogued here a small number of works to which no author's name is appended and of which the authorship has not been traced. Any catalogue of these which should be useful would be a thematic catalogue; it is hoped that these anonymous works will be catalogued thematically in a Second Part, which will appear in fasciculi. There is also a considerable number of printed books, many of which are of great interest. There are, however, few volumes of which specimens are not to be found elsewhere, so that the need for a published catalogue is less pressing. There is an ancient manuscript catalogue which was copied in an elaborate fashion on vellum by the Rev. H. E. Havergal, M.A., formerly Chaplain, in the years 1845–7. So far as I am aware, this copy professed to be, and was, a copy and nothing else. While the late Professor York Powell occupied the office of Librarian the books were very carefully put in order. Bindings were repaired, unbound volumes were beautifully bound, loose sheets, of which there were a large number, were sorted and their contents identified. For some of this work we had the help of Sir John Stainer, then Professor of Music in the University. Under Professor Powell's successor, Mr. F. J. Haverfield, now Camden Professor of Ancient History, the books were rearranged and the Catalogue revised and brought up to date. It was then decided, on the proposal of the present Librarian, Mr. H. W. Blunt, to print the Catalogue as it stood, in order that musical scholars might know generally what is to be found in the Library. At this stage the Governing Body had the great good fortune of securing the services of Mr. G. E. P. Arkwright, a scholar of the first rank in music of the sixteenth and seventeenth centuries. Mr. Arkwright has gone carefully over the whole Collection and verified all the entries in the Catalogue. But this is not all. In the old Catalogues there was a very long list of anonymous works: by means of his great knowledge of the period Mr. Arkwright has succeeded in tracing the large majority of these works, and they now appear under the name of their composers. I take this opportunity of offering to Mr. Arkwright the most sincere thanks of myself and my colleagues for his invaluable help.

It may not be out of place to add a few words upon the Collection itself. It represents mainly the taste and enthusiasm of one man, H. Aldrich, Dean, 1689–1712. Aldrich was a man of many gifts and his name is well known. It is hardly necessary to refer to his works in Logic and Theology or to his skill in architecture: we are concerned with him, at present, only as a musician. It was an age of congratulatory verses and odes. Every royal visitor and every occasion of public importance, as well as the annual Act, produced a rich crop of these compositions. Aldrich wrote the music for several of these occasions: for the Encaenia, 1672, 1674, 1675; for the entertainment of the Duke of York, 1683 (*Wood's Life and Times*, O.H.S., vol. ii. 248, 258, 319, iii. 52). But these were not the only occasions when music was required. There was, of course, the music of the Church; also, under the Statutes then in operation, the Choragus was ordered to provide a weekly concert, and it is plain from Wood and Hearne that a great deal of music must have been performed in Oxford at this time. Such concerts will, no doubt, account for a large amount of the music owned by Aldrich; but it is also plain that he was a real student of music, and collected not only for purposes of performance, but also as a connoisseur. In his will, after bequeathing his music to Christ Church, he goes on: 'I make it my request to the Dean and Chapter of the said

Church that they will be pleased to take such care of my Prints and books of Musick that they may not be exposed to common usage nor to any man without their leave and appointment, because they are things of value in themselves and to be found in very few Libraries.'

The only considerable addition to the books came from the library of Richard Goodson, organist of the Cathedral and Professor of Music in the University from 1682–1718. I have failed to discover any detailed information about this man. His period as organist coincided very largely with Aldrich's residence in Christ Church. Aldrich was Tutor and Censor, then Canon, before he became Dean in 1689. The tastes of the two men must have been in close agreement. Goodson, like Aldrich, wrote music for the Oxford Acts and for the services of the Church; but though Aldrich in G and certain anthems are still heard here and elsewhere, Goodson's compositions have gone out of use. Yet he would seem—if, for once, we may trust the language of an epitaph—to have had a high reputation in his day for music, and, if I am not putting too much weight upon the words of the epitaph, for personal charm:

H. S. E.

Ricardus Goodson

Hujus Eccles: Organista

Hujus Academ: Mus: Praelector

Utrique Deliciae et Decus.

Since the days of Goodson there has been no large addition to the Library. The interest in music prevailing in England shortly after the Restoration lasted throughout the eighteenth century, but without producing any considerable musician at Christ Church. It then passed away altogether, and for a long period of years music was regarded in higher academic circles as an eccentric if not a mischievous pursuit. This view would not lead either to the extension of the Collection, or even to the filling up of lacunae. The books have been used by various workers in the field of musical history. Dr. Burney (*Hist. of Music*, vol. iii, p. 66, note) speaks of the importance of the Collection, and then adds : 'To these valuable books I have not only been honoured with free access by the Rev. Dean and Chapter, but allowed, in the most liberal manner, to take away many of the most curious in the collection out of the library, for a considerable time, in order to consult and make extracts from them at my leisure.' I may perhaps, without disrespect to Dr. Burney, venture to suggest that this liberal policy, if extensively pursued, may account for some of the gaps. Until recent years the music in this as in other Cathedrals was performed from manuscript part-books. These are now superseded by printed copies. The old Cathedral-books, which have many features of interest—especially a series of chants written before the present fixed arrangement of bars was adopted—are now deposited in the Music Library. Nearly all the works outside the period of Aldrich and the Goodsons are in these volumes. Among these is the volume containing chants throughout the month, and a number of anthems by Crotch, mainly in the hand-writing of Dr. Crotch himself. He was organist here from 1790–1807.

To note all the points of interest in these books would take me far beyond the limits of a Preface. I will confine myself to quoting the note in Rogers' handwriting on the fly-sheet of MS. 21 :

> Beñ. Rogers his booke Aug. 18 1673 ·
> and p̄sented me by Mr. John Playford Stationer
> in the Temple · London ·
> This Score-booke was done formerly
> by that rare musician Mr. Orlando Gibbons
> and this book is of great value to a composer.

The Collection throws some light on the organists of Christ Church and their achievements. It contains certain works by J. Taverner, who was master of the children in Cardinal College, and who was certainly able to play the organ. He was playing at the Evensong on February 21, 1528, when the Cardinal's Commissary arrived to inquire into the orthodoxy of the College.[1]   In Christ Church there was a choir consisting of boys and men, with a master of the choristers, and the receipts for their payments appear in the Disbursement Books every quarter [2]: but there does not seem to have been an organist before the beginning of the seventeenth century: and there is no evidence of expenditure upon the organ. It is probable that the master of the choristers played the organ also. The boys have a master to teach them grammar and also music: the same person usually performs both these functions. In March, 1605, the word 'organista' occurs for the first time, and the signature attached to it is that of Leonard Major. Leonard Major signs in June, 1605, the receipt of a sum for the purchase of instruments. In 1608 Mr. W. Stonnard appears as organist for the first time, together with a blower. A setting of the Magnificat and Nunc Dimittis of his appears in the Catalogue. He died in 1629, and was succeeded by Edw. Lowe. This gentleman passed through the Commonwealth. Payments for the organist and blower disappear in 1644 and 1645, the books which alone survive for this period, but in 1659 E. Lowe reappears. He held office till 1682. A considerable number of his compositions is to be found in the Library. After E. Lowe came W. Husbands, who held office till 1692. His name also is in the Catalogue, but he seems to have arranged the compositions of other men rather than composed on his own account. Then follows Richard Goodson, the friend of Aldrich, and part-founder of the Collection; he is succeeded in 1718 by his son, also called Richard Goodson. The elder but not the younger is represented in the Collection. In 1741 R. Church succeeded R. Goodson the younger, but he also seems to have left no compositions to the Cathedral. In 1776 T. Norris was appointed organist, a man with a

---

[1] See Foxe's *Acts and Monuments*, ii, p. 523, ed. 1641 ; Grove's *Dictionary of Music*, vol. v, p. 30, art. 'Taverner', by G. E. P. Arkwright.

[2] The Disbursement Books are kept in the Treasury. The earliest book is dated 1577. There are large gaps during the broken times of the Commonwealth, but with this exception the series is complete.

distinguished record as a singer: one anthem and perhaps three chants represent his achievement, so far as the Collection is concerned. Then, at the age of fifteen, W. Crotch became organist of Christ Church, the most distinguished musician who had yet held the post. His avocations, besides his work in the Cathedral, were numerous, and he moved to London in 1807, still retaining the Professorship of Music. W. Cross was his successor, followed in 1825 by W. Marshall. Both were undistinguished. In 1846 came W. Corfe, son of the organist of Salisbury, who held office till 1882, and is in the recollection of many persons still living. Though a player of very limited resources and by no means a prolific composer, he was a fine musician: old-fashioned in his musical education, he learnt to understand modern music, including that of Brahms. His three successors, Dr. C. H. Lloyd (1882–92), Dr. B. Harwood (1892–1909), and Mr. H. G. Ley, are still with us.

T. B. S.

INTRODUCTION

This Catalogue of the MS. music preserved in the Christ Church Library is based upon that made in 1845–7 by the Rev. H. E. Havergal. In Mr. Havergal's Catalogue, which was never printed, the works whose authors are known were arranged under an alphabetical list of Composers. There were also four lists of anonymous compositions, (i) Sacred music with English words; (ii) with foreign words; (iii) Secular music with English words; (iv) with foreign words; arranged according to the alphabetical order of their first words. The anonymous instrumental works were not catalogued at all.

The alphabetical list of Composers' names has been revised and remodelled, and is now printed. But it is felt that lists of words of anonymous compositions are of very little use, and these are reserved for future volumes: it is hoped that a series of thematic catalogues may be issued, beginning with the anonymous Italian cantatas.

The musical MSS. in this Library are not all of equal interest. Some of them, such as the fine Set of Part-books, 984–8; or the Orlando Gibbons autograph album, 21; or the Virginal Book, 1113; are of the highest importance. Others are merely compressed Organ Parts made by nineteenth-century organists from accessible printed collections, and are of little value. Dean Aldrich's own MS. copies of old English music (of which the Library contains many volumes) must not be accepted as good authorities; for it was his practice to alter them freely, so much so that it has been thought best to catalogue many of them as ' adaptations ' under the name of Aldrich.

Whenever I have found that any of the compositions catalogued have been published, I have noted the fact for purposes of identification. In many cases no doubt the printed versions may prove to differ considerably from the MS. copies. It must not be assumed that all the other works are unprinted. I have only noted those which I happen myself to have seen in print.

The principal printed collections to which I refer are the following:

Arnold. Dr. Samuel Arnold's collection of Cathedral Music, edited by Edward F. Rimbault, 1842.

Barnard. Selected Church Musick, 1641.

Boyce and *Warren's Boyce.* Cathedral Music, 1760–73. Joseph Warren's Edition, 1849, contains anthems and services not found in the original edition.

Burney. A General History of Music, 1776–89.

Cath. Mag. The Cathedral Magazine, or Divine Harmony, 1775.

Chappell. Old English Popular Music, edited by H. Ellis Wooldridge, 1893.

Clifford. Divine Services and Anthems, 1663: 2nd Edition 1664. [A collection of words only.]

Cope. Anthems by Eminent Composers of the English Church, edited by the Rev. W. H. Cope, 1849–51.

The Fitzwilliam Virginal Book edited by W. Barclay Squire and J. A. Fuller Maitland.

Goss and Turle. Services Ancient and Modern.

Hawkins. A General History of the Science and Practice of Music, 1776.

Jebb. The Choral Responses and Litanies of the United Church of England and Ireland, 1847–57.

Marshall. Dr. William Marshall's Collection of Cathedral Services.

Motett Soc. Collection of Ancient Church Music Printed by the Motett Society.

O. E. Ed. The Old English Edition, 1889–1902.

Ouseley (i) Cathedral Services, 1853.
    (ii) Sacred compositions of Orlando Gibbons, 1873.

Page. Harmonia Sacra, 1800.

The Parish Choir, 1846–51.

Rimbault. Cathedral Music.

Squire. Purcell's Harpsichord Music, Purcell Society, 1895, edited by W. Barclay Squire.

Besides these authorities, I have made free use of the books of reference, dictionaries, catalogues, histories, and musical journals, without which no work of this kind can be undertaken. I mention in particular The Dictionary of National Biography; *Foster's* Alumni Oxonienses; *Grove's* Dictionary of Music and Musicians, 1904–10; *Eitner's* Quellen-Lexicon, 1900–4; The King's Musick, by the Rev. *H. C. De Lafontaine*, 1909; A History of English Cathedral Music by *John S. Bumpus*; A History of English Music by *Henry Davey*; *Rimbault's* Old Cheque-Book of the Chapel Royal, 1872; and his Bibliotheca Madrigaliana, 1847; Cathedral Organists by *John E. West*, 1899; Degrees in Music by *C. F. Abdy Williams*; Alessandro Scarlatti by *E. J. Dent*, 1905; Luigi Rossi by *A. Wotquenne*, 1909;

Alessandro Stradella, by *H. Hess*, 1906. The British Museum Catalogue of Printed Music, 1912, and the Royal College of Music Catalogue of Printed Music, 1909 by *W. Barclay Squire*; The Catalogue of MS. Music in the British Museum 1906–9, by *A. Hughes-Hughes*; The Library of Congress Catalogue of Opera Librettos, 1914 by *O. G. T. Sonneck*; The Catalogue de la Bibliothèque du Conservatoire Royal de Musique de Bruxelles, by *A. Wotquenne*; The Catalogue du Fonds de Musique Ancienne de la Bibliothèque Nationale by *J. Ecorcheville*; The Catalogue of Music in the Fitzwilliam Museum, by *J. A. Fuller Maitland* and *A. H. Mann*. The *Rivista Musicale Italiana*; The *Sammelbände der Internationalen Musik-Gesellschaft*; The *Musical Antiquary*; and Mr. F. G. Edwards's articles in the *Musical Times*.

I have received much help in the course of preparing this Catalogue, and I have pleasure in gratefully acknowledging my obligations in particular to Mr. E. J. Dent, who put at my disposal his lists of Scarlatti's Songs and has looked out references for me, and identified music at Cambridge and at Berlin. I have also to express my indebtedness to Professor Ch. Van den Borren of the Université nouvelle de Bruxelles, who has identified some music for me and advised me as to MSS. at Brussels; to Dr. Hugo Leichtentritt, who collated some Scarlatti MSS. at Berlin; Cav. Livi and Monsieur André Pirro have given me valuable help in the endeavour to identify compositions by Carissimi and by Pietro Cornet. I have consulted Mr. W. J. Lawrence also with regard to some of the seventeenth and and eighteenth century plays of which the music is found in the Library.

There are some contractions used in this Catalogue which need explanation.

v. = voices: 4 v. = for 4 voices.
A. = Alto : T. = Tenor : B. = Bass.
S. = Soprano : Tr. = Treble.
V. A. = Verse Anthem : F. A. = Full Anthem.
V. and Chos. = Verse and Chorus.
Te D., Bte., Btus., Jub., Ky., Sctus., Glo., Mag., N. Dim., Cant. D. Mis. = Te Deum, Benedicite, Benedictus, Jubilate, Kyrie, Sanctus, Gloria, Magnificat, Nunc Dimittis, Cantate and Deus Misereatur.
Sc. = Score : Sep. = Separate parts.
B. M. = British Museum.
R. C. M. = Royal College of Music.

G. E. P. A.

ALCOCK (John). 1715–1806. Mus. Doc. Organist of Lichfield
1749–60.

Service in E mi. Published in 1753.
Te D., Jub., Ky., Creed, Mag., N. Dim. Score   **41**
Two Chants (the first also in **1229**, without name) **1226**
Thirteen Chants (2 with name, 11 with initials J. A.) **1229**

ALDRICH (Henry). 1647–1710. D.D. Dean of Ch. Ch. 1689.

SERVICES.

Service in E mi. 4 v. Bte., Jub., Ky., Creed. Score **50**
  The same, with 'If the Lord himself' and Mag. and
   N. Dim. A. and B. parts only **785**
  Benedicite from the same (unfinished). Score **19**
Service in F. 2–5 v. Te D., Jub. (two versions), Ky., Creed, Mag.,
   N. Dim. Score **19**
  Sep. parts. (A. T. B. only) **1220–4**
  A. and B. Chorus parts (incomplete) **1188–9**
  Organ part, without Mag. and N. Dim. **1230**
Service in G. 4 v. Printed *c.* 1690 without Sctus. and Glor.; and
 in *Boyce*. Sctus. and Glor. in *Ouseley*.
  Te D., Jub., Ky., Creed, Sctus., Glor., Mag., N. Dim.
  Score **19, 50**
  The same without Sctus. and Glor. Score **15**
  Organ parts **1225, 1228**
Service in A. 4 v. *Arnold*.
  Te D., Jub., Ky., Creed, Cant., Deus Mis. Score
   19, 50
  Te D. (unfinished). Score **1111**
  Cantate and Deus Mis. Score **15**
  Organ part, without Ky. and Creed **1228**
Three Single Chants. 4 v. Score **48**
  The 1st and 3rd of these, Organ part **1226**
Another Single Chant. Organ part **1226**

ANTHEMS.

All people that on earth. V. A. Adapted from Tallis. *Arnold,*
Motett Soc., &c.
  Scores **11, 16 (2 versions), 614**
  Sep. T. and B. only **1220–4**
  Organ parts **1230, 1235**

B

ALDRICH (Henry)—*continued.*

Behold in heav'n. V. A. (from Carissimi) cf. B. M. Addl. MS.
17840. Ascribed to Blow, in late hand, in **12** and **16**.

    Score   **12, 16, 614**

    Sep. A. T. (verse and Chos.), B. (verse and Chos.)

    1220–4

Behold now praise the Lord. 5 v. (Adapted from ? Palestrina) *Cope.*

    Score   **19**

    Organ parts   **1228, 1230**

Be not wroth. 5 v. Freely adapted from Byrd's Civitas sancti tui
in *Sacrae Cantiones*, 1589.

    Scores   **16, 614**

    Sep. parts, A. T. B. only   **1220–4**

    Organ part   **1230**

Blessed is the man, V. A.: probably an adaptation by Aldrich.

    Scores   **12, 16, 614**

By the waters of Babylon. 6 v. (Adaptation. Ascribed to
Farrant in a late hand in 16). *Cope.* Score   **11, 16**

    Four-part version. Score   **614**

    Organ part   **1230**

    An anonymous version, slightly different, with Gloria
    Patri. Sep. A. T. B. only   **1220–4**

Call to remembrance. 4 v. (Adapted from Farrant with added
verse, O remember not.) **Score**   **11, 16, 614**

    Organ   **1230**

Comfort ye my people. V. A. for A. T. B. and Chos.

    Score   **19**

For Sion's sake. V. A. (Adapted from Carissimi.)

    Score   **12, 16, 614**

Give ear O Lord. F. A. 4 v. (? Adaptation.)

    Score   **11, 19**

    Sep. parts   **521–4**

    Sep. parts, A. T. B. only   **1220–4**

    Organ part   **1230**

    Fragment of Studies for same   **1188–9**

Give the king thy judgements. Bass Solo and Chos. One page
of this anthem was printed by Aldrich as part of an intended
publication, fol.: no place nor date   **1208**

    Score   **15, 19**

God is our hope. 5 v. *Page,* &c. Score   **19**

    Organ part   **1230**

God is our refuge. T. T. and Chos. ? Adaptation. Score

    12, 16, 614

Haste thee O Lord my God. 2–6 v. (Adapted from Carissimi.)

    Score   **16, 614**

Have mercy upon me. T. Solo and Chos. Printed by Aldrich as
part of an intended publication   **1208**

    Score   **19**

ALDRICH (Henry)—*continued.*

Hide not thou thy face. 5 v. (Adapted from Farrant.) Score
    11, 16

    Sep. parts, A. T. B. only   **1220–4**
    Arranged for 4 v. Score   **614**
    Organ part of same, as in **614**   **1230**

Hold not thy tongue. 4 v. (Adapted from Palestrina's *Nativitas tua.*) Score   **11, 614**
    Score, two versions   **16**
    Organ part   **1230**

I am come into my garden. 2 v. (S. and B). Score initialled H. A.   **18**

I am well pleased. V. A. for A. T. B. and Chos. (Adapted from Carissimi.) *Arnold.*
    Score   **12, 16, 614**
    Organ part   **1226**

If the Lord himself. V. A. Score   **19**

(In **19** a later hand has written 'Dr. Child' above this Anthem. Child's setting, however, is quite different. All the contents of **19** are by Aldrich.)
    A. and B. Chos. parts only   **785**

I look for the Lord. 5 v. Freely adapted from Tallis's Absterge Domine in *Cantiones*, 1575. Score   **11, 16, 614**
    A. T. B. only   **1220–4**
    Organ   **1230**
    Sep., differing from above (twice)   **510–4**

I waited patiently. Sopr. Solo and Chos. Score   **15, 19**

I will exalt thee. V. A. with Instruments. Score   **19**
    Violin part   **1142**

I will love thee. Bass Solo and Chos. Score   **19, 22**

My heart is fixed. 4 v. (Adapted from Palestrina's *Nos autem gloriari.*) Score   **11, 16, 614**
    Organ part   **1230**

Not unto us. 4 v. (Adapted from Farrant and Lawes). *Arnold*, &c.
    Score   **48**
    Organ part   **1230**

O give thanks. 6 v. Printed *c.* 1690 : *Boyce*, &c. Score   **19**
    Second Treble part only   **683**
    Organ part   **1230**
    Fragments and sketches   **1188–9**

O God the King of Glory. 4 v. (Adapted from Palestrina's *O rex gloriæ.*) Score   **11, 16, 614**
    Sep. parts   **521–4**
    Sep. parts wanting Cantus   **1220–4**
    Organ part   **1230**

O God thou art my God. T. Solo and Chos. Score   **15, 19**

O how amiable. V. A. S. S. and Chos. (Adapted from Carissimi.)
    Score   **12, 16, 22, 614**

ALDRICH (Henry)—*continued.*

O Lord God of my salvation. (Adapted from Palestrina, cf. B. M. Addl. MS. 31399.) Score   **48**
      Organ part   **1230**

O Lord grant the Queen. 5 v. Score   **783**
      Organ part   **1230**

O Lord I bow the knees. (Altered from Mundy.) Score   **16, 614**
      Organ part   **1230**

O Lord I have heard. V. A. Score   **19, 22**

O Lord I will praise. V. A. (Adapted from Carissimi.)
    Score   **12, 16, 614**

O Lord my God. V. A. (Altered from Bull, q. v.) *Boyce.*
    Score   **16, 614**

O Lord our Governor. S. Solo initialled H. A.   **18**
      The same (with different Gloria for 4 v.) Score   **19**

O praise the Lord all ye heathen. 4 v. *Arnold.* Score   **11, 15, 19**
      Organ parts   **1230, 1235**

O pray for the peace. V. A. (Adapted from Carissimi.)
    Score   **12, 16, 614**

O sing unto the Lord. S. Solo and Chos. Score   **19**

Out of the deep. 4 v. *Boyce,* &c. Score   **11, 15, 19**
      Sep. parts, wanting Cantus   **1220–4**
      Organ parts   **1230, 1235**

Praise the Lord, O ye his servants. V. A. Score   **15, 19**
      Treble voice part without Gloria at end   **1114**

Sing unto the Lord, O ye saints. 4 v. Score   **19**
      Organ part (imperfect)   **1230**

The eye of the Lord. F. A. 4 v. (Adapted from Palestrina's *Jesus junxit se.*) Score   **11, 16** (two versions), **614**
      Organ part   **1230**

The Lord is king. S. Solo and Chos. Score   **19, 22**

Thy beauty O Israel. V. A. (Arranged from Wise, q. v.) *Boyce.*
    Score   **614**

Unto thee, O Lord. V. A. Score   **15** (two versions), **19**

We have a strong city. V. A. for A. T. B. and Chos. Score   **19**

We have heard. 4 v. (Adapted from Palestrina's *Doctor bonus.*)
    Arnold. Score   **11, 16, 614**
      Organ part   **1230**

Who's this that comes. V. A. Score   **19**
      Imperfect copy, beginning 'Brought me salvation' and differing considerably from **19**   **15**

Why art thou so vexed? 4 v. (Adapted from Palestrina's *Ave Maria.*) Score   **11, 16, 614**
      Sep. parts   **521–4**
      Sep. parts, wanting Cantus   **1220–4**
      Organ part   **1230**

O bone Jesu. 4 v. (S. S. A. B.) Score initialled H. A.   **18**

Salvator mundi. (S. S. B.) Score initialled H. A.   **18**

ALDRICH (Henry)—*continued*.

SECULAR WORKS.

Consurge tandem
Iam satis somno, 1679 } Songs for the Oxford Act. 1–4 v. With
Revixit Io Carolus   } overtures and instr. parts.   Score   **619**

Conveniunt doctæ sorores { Act Song performed in the Oxford
Hic sede Carolus   { Theatre, July 7, 1682. 6 v. With
                         { overtures and instr. parts.

    Sep. parts   **1127**
(This is probably by Aldrich, in whose writing it seems to be.)
Philomela prævia temporis. 3 v. (S. S. B.) Score initialled H. A. **17**
Good, good indeed. A catch on Tobacco. 4 v. (Printed in
 Catch that catch can, 1682)   **598**
O the bonny Christ Church bells   **1003**
Suites of short pieces in 2 parts   **90–1**
   Nine pieces in A mi., of which 1, 6, and 9 have the
    name Mr. Oldridge or Alderidg; five pieces in G mi.,
    the last bearing the name Mr. Oldridg; four pieces
    in C, the 2nd and 4th by Mr. Oldredge.
Papers prepared for a treatise on Music   **1187**
[See also under *Alsop: Blow: Bull: Byrd: Farrant* (*R.*): *Goodson:*
 Mundy: Palestrina: Pseudocarissimi: Tallis: R. White: Wise.]

ALISON (Richard), fl. 1592–1606.

My prime of youth, Pt. I }
The spring is past, Pt. II } Treble solo   **439**
   From *An Howres Recreation*, 1606.

ALOYSIUS (Giovanni Battista Aloisi) of Bologna. Published
 between 1628 and 1640.

Four Motets from *Cœlestis Parnassus*, 1628.
   Basso continuo only   **880**
Attollite portas. 4 v.
Cantate Domino. 4 v.
Dulcissima Christi. 4 v.
Impetum inimicorum. 4 v.

ALSOP (Anthony) of Ch. Ch., d. 1726, for whom see *Dict. Nat.*
 Biogr. Probably author of the words only.

Britannia, a song written for the Oxford Act, 1693, beginning
 'Dum Mosa torpet.' 'Supposed to be adapted to music of
 Carissimi,' ? by Aldrich. 1–4 v. Score   **619**

AMBROSE (John). A 16th-century writer, known only by an instru-
 mental piece in B. M. Roy. MSS. Appx., No. 58.

Fancy, for keyboard instrument   **1034**

AMNER (John), Mus. Bac.   Organist of Ely, 1610–41.
  Consider all yee passers by.   V. A. for 5 v.   Sep. parts wanting
    Bass   56–60
  I am for peace.   V. A. for 5 v.   Sep. parts wanting Bass   56–60
  Lord in thy wrath.   V. A.   5 v.   Organ part   6
  My shepperd is the livinge Lorde.   V. A.   6 v.   Organ part   6
  O magnifye the Lorde our God.   V. A.   Organ part   6
  The king shall rejoyce.   V. A.   Organ part   6

ANERIO (Felice), Composer to the Papal Chapel, 1594–1602.
  The nightingale recountinge.   Madrigal for 4 v.   Sep. parts
                                                            1074–7

  Why sitt we so deiected.   (Adapted from ' Se darmi à tutte ' from
    Canzonette, 1586).   Sep. parts   1074–7

ARNE (Thomas Augustine), Mus. Doc.   1710–78.
  Vain is Beauty's gaudy flow'r.   A song in the oratorio *Judith*   1111

ARNOLD (Samuel), Mus. Doc.   1740–1802.   Organist of West-
    minster Abbey.
  Single Chant   1226

ASOLA or **ASULA** (Giovanni Matteo), of Verona.   Chapel Master
    at Treviso, 1578; and at Vicenza, 1581.
  Reioyce ye holye Martyrs.   3 v.   Sep.   750–3

ASTON or **ASHTON** (Hugh), fl. in the early 16th century.
  ' Hugh Ashton's Maske,' in 4 parts, wanting Bass   979–83
  Probably a composition on this ground by Whytbrooke, whose
    name is attached to the contra tenor part.

ASTORGA (Baron Emmanuele d').   See *Scarlatti* (*Alessandro*) for
    Cantata ' Deh per mercè.'

B. (J.) probably John Bannister, q. v.
  Ayre ;   In Nomine fantasia ;   Pavin (not in Alto nor Bassus
    Books) for Instruments.   5 parts.   Sep.   473–8
  Air, or perhaps 4 airs, by J. B.   Violin part only.   1025–7

B. (L. G.)
  Three Chants   1226

BACCUSI (Hippolito), Chapel Master at Verona, 1572 ; and at
    Mantua, 1584 ; d. at Verona, 1609.
  Fly hence, ye shades of night. Canzonet.   3 v.   Treble part
    only   742

BAILEY (   ).
  Double Chant   1226

BALTZAR or BALTAZAR (Thomas), *c.* 1630–63.　Violinist.　A native of Lübeck; came to England in 1656; was in Oxford in 1658 (cf. A. Wood's *Life and Times*).

A Set of Tunings.　Two Almans and a Sarabrand.　Violin part only　　**1125**

BANISTER (John), 1630–79.　'Chief of His Majesty's Violins,' 1663.

Part of the incidental music to Katherine Philips's tragedy, *Pompey*, 1663.　Banister's name is attached to the first song only, but probably the rest is his also　　**350**
From lasting and unclouded day.　Sopr. Solo.　After the 3rd Act.
Proud monument of Royal Dust.　Sopr. Solo.　After the 4th Act.
Ascend the Throne.　Sopr. Solo.　　　　　　} After the
Then after all the blood.　Chorus, Sopr. and Bass only.} 5th Act.
The bread is all baked.　3 v.　From D'Avenant's comedy, *The Man's the Master*, 1669　　**23**
[? Begon all fruitless joys　　**350**
This seems to be a version, much altered, of Banister's song in B. M. Addl. MS. 19759]
Ten sets of Brawles, Dances, Airs, &c., for strings, of which one is called 'The Musick at the Bath'; and one set for trumpets. Sep. parts　　**1183**
Airs, &c., for violin.　1st V. part only.　11 airs or sets　　**361**
　　　　　　6 airs or sets　　**362**
Grounds in G mi. (Tr. Tr. B.); F and B♮ (Tr. and B.) [formerly 1125]　　**1183**
The G mi. Ground.　1st Tr. only　　**1025–7**
Saraband for Harpsichord　　**1003**
[See *B.* (*J.*)]

BAPTIST, or BABTIST.　Probably Jean-Baptiste Lully, q.v.; though Gio. Battista Draghi, organist to Catharine of Braganza, was also known in England as Signor Baptist or Baptista.

Tune for violin (violin part only), 'Mr. Baptist'　　**362**
Tune for violin (violin part only), 'Babtist'　　**1066**
Three tunes for recorder.　Treble and Bass.　'Mr. Baptist.'
　　　　　　　　　　　1118 and **1121**
[See *Batis.*]

BARE.　Probably intended for La Barre, q. v.
Corant for Harpsichord　　**1236**

BARRETT (John), *c.* 1674–*c.* 1735.　Music master at Christ's Hospital.
Corant for Harpsichord　　**46**

BARTORELLI (Benedetto).　A 17th-century writer.
Basta amor.　Cantata for Sopr. Solo　　**947**

BASSANI (Giovanni Battista). *c.* 1657–1716. Born at Padua. Chapel master to the Cathedral of Ferrara. Died at Bergamo.

The Motets marked * are from his Opera 8, *Metri sacri resi armonici*, Bologna, 1690. The MS. 1124 contains only short extracts, apparently chosen for purposes of study, or teaching.

Advolate fideles. 2 v. S. S.	48
*Aligeri amores. Voice and Bass only	763
Alto voice only	389
1st and 2nd violins and violone, sep.	1154
*Ave verax honor. Voice and Bass only	763
*Eja tubæ. Voice and Bass only	763
1st and 2nd violin parts (loose)	1154
Esurientes venite. 2 v. S. B.	48, 1204
Gaude alma dilecta. S. S. B. extract without words	1124
*In caligine. Voice and Bass only	763
With 3 instrumental parts in score	23
1st and 2nd violin and violone parts, sep.	1154
*In hoc mundo. Voice and Bass only	763
With 2 instrumental parts in score	23
1st and 2nd violin and violone parts, sep.	1154
In sole lucente. S. and B. without words (extract)	1124
Lætare lætare. S. S. B. without words (extract)	1124
O donum. S. S. B. without words (extract)	1124
O sacrum. S. S. B. without words (extract)	1124
O splendida dies. 2 v. S. B.	48
*Pompæ vanæ. Voice and Bass only	763
1st and 2nd violin and violone parts, sep.	1154
Pulchra es amica mea. 2 v. S. S.	48
Quando tandem sponse care. S. and B. without words (extract)	1124
*Quid arma, quid bella. Voice and Bass only	763
With 3 instrumental parts in score	23
Violone part only	690
Ride tellus gaude caelum. 2 v. S. B.	48
Sub umbra noctis. S. S. B. without words (extract)	1124
Suenturati miei pensieri. Cantata for Sopr. Solo	958

Sonata in A mi. Vo. 1 and 2, Vcello. and Basso. (The first Sonata from *Suonate a due, tre instrumenti*, [&c.] Opera Quinta, Anversa, 1691.) Score   3

BASSANO (Hieronymo), probably Jerome, son of Anthony Bassano or Bassani, who came to England *c.* 1539. Jerome appears as one of the King's Musicians, 1603–30.

Four fancies in 5 parts. Sep.   716–20

BATIS. Probably for Baptist, q. v.

Almaine, Corant, and Sarabant for Harpsichord, in D mi.   1177

BATTEN (Adrian). Organist of St. Paul's, ? 1624 ; d. about 1637.
Morning and Evening Service in Dorian Mode. *Goss and Turle*,
  Te D., Jub., Ky., Creed, Mag., N. Dim. Organ parts **437, 438**
  (In **438**, the Jub. is headed Benedictus, no doubt by mistake.)
The same without Ky. and Creed. Organ part   **1227**
The same. Te D., Jub., Ky., Creed, Mag., N. Dim. Bass only **1012**
'Long Service.' Te D., Jub., Ky., Creed, Mag., N. Dim. Sep.
  parts wanting Cantus   **1220–4**
Preces and 'first Psalmes' (Ps. xx) ; '2ᵈ Psalmes for Easter Day'
  (Ps. xxi) ; '3ᵈ Psalmes for yᵉ 27 of March' ; '4ᵗʰ Psalmes'
  (Ps. lxvii) ; '5ᵗʰ Psalmes' (Ps. cxlv) ; '6ᵗʰ Psalmes for Whit-
  sunday' (Ps. xlv). Bass part only   **1148**

ANTHEMS.

Deliver us O God. 4 v. *Boyce*. Sep. T. and B. only   **1220–4**
  Organ parts   **438, 1228**
Haste thee O God. 4 v. *Barnard, Cope*.
  Sep. T. and B. only   **1220–4**
  Bass part only   **1012**
  Organ parts   **437**, imperfect at end ; **438**
Hear my prayer. 5 v. *Boyce*. Organ part   **1228**
Hide not thou thy face. *Barnard*. Organ part   **437**
Lord we beseech thee. 4 v. *Barnard*. *Parish Choir*.
  Organ part   **437**
O Lord thou hast searched. V. A. Organ part   **6**
O praise the Lord. 4 v. *Barnard, Boyce*, &c.
  Sep. parts, A. T. B. only   **1220–4**
  Organ parts   **437, 438, 1228**
Out of the deep. 4 v. (not *Barnard's*). Bass part only **1012**
When the Lord turned. 4 v. *Barnard, Cope*.
  Bass part only   **1012**

BATTISHILL (Jonathan). 1738–1801.
Three chants   **1226**

BAWDWINE (John). Perhaps the same as John Baldwin, a singing
  man from Windsor, who was sworn Gent. of the Chapel Royal
  1598, and died 1615. His name appears as that of the copyist
  of many MSS. The set of part-books, 979–83, which bear the
  initials I. B. stamped on the covers, may have belonged to him.
Pater noster. 5 v. (?) Wanting the Tenor Book   **979–83**
Redime domine. 5 v. (?) Wanting the Tenor Book   **979–83**
A fancy in 3 parts. Wanting the Tenor Book   **979–83**
A fancy in 3 parts, called 'Coockow as me walked'. Wanting the
  Tenor Book   **979–83**

BECKIT or BECKET (Philip). One of the King's Musicians,
  1660–78. He is named both among the Violins and the Wind
  Instruments.
Twelve Airs, &c., in 4 parts. Treble only.   **1066**

BECKWITH (John Christmas). 1750–1809. Mus. Doc. Organist
of Norwich Cathedral.
Four Chants   **1226**

BENITTI (?) (   ).   An unknown composer of the 17th century.
Occhi belli.   Cantata for Sopr. Solo   **948**

BENNET (John), fl. 1599–1614.
Oh God of gods.   V. A. for 5 v.   Sep. wanting Bass   **56–60**
       Organ part   **67**
All creatures now.   Madrigal.   5 v.   From *The Triumphs of Oriana.*
Score without words   **33**
Venus birds.   Treble Solo and Bass.   (Cf. B. M. Add. MS. 17786,
&c.)   **439**
Ye restles thoughts.   Two Treble parts only.   From the *Madrigals,*
1599   **740, 742**

BENNET (S.).
Double chant in G   **1226**

BEVIN (Elway).   Organist of Bristol, 1589; Gent. of the Chapel
Royal, 1605; from which posts he is said to have been expelled
as a Papist in 1637.
'Short' service in Dorian mode.   *Barnard, Boyce.*   Te D., Bdtus.,
Ky., Creed, Mag., N. Dim.   Score   **42, 1002**
Sep. parts, wanting Cantus   **1220–4**
The same, without Ky. and Creed.   Organ part   **1227**
The same, Te D. and Bdtus. only.   Organ part   **438**
The same, Te D., Bdtus., Ky., Creed, with different Mag. and
N. Dim.   Organ part   **1001**
Venite to same.   Sep. parts.   A. T. and B. only   **1220–4**
Mag. and N. Dim., 'Mr. Bevin's Gimill.'   Sep. parts A. T. B. only
                                                         1220–4
Browning.[1]   For instruments in 3 parts.   Treble and Tenor only.
                                                          979–83

BIRCHENSHA (John), fl. 1651–72.   He lived at Dublin in the
service of the Earl of Kildare till 1641.   He was a teacher of
music in London about 1651, and wrote on the theory of music.
Twelve pieces for Violin and Bass and Organ.
       Vo. and Bass.   Sep. parts   **1016–7**
       Organ part   **781**

---

[1] A composition founded on the tune called 'Browning': see Chappell's *Old
English Popular Music,* 1893, i. 155.

BISHOP (John). 1665–1737. Organist of Winchester Cathedral.
Service in D.

Te D., Bdtus., Ky., Creed, Cantate, Deus Mis. Score	**42**
Cantate and Deus Mis. only. Organ part	**1231**
Bow down thine ear. Organ part	**1235**
Call to remembrance. Sep. parts wanting Çantus	**1220–4**
Organ part	**1234**
O be joyful. Sep. parts wanting Cantus	**1220–4**
Tenor only	**1219**
Organ part	**1234**
O how amiable. Organ part	**1235**

BLOW (John). 1648–1708. Mus. Doc. Master of the Children of
the Chapel Royal, 1674. Organist of Westminster Abbey.

SERVICES.

Service in A. 4 v. *Boyce*. Te D., Jub., Ky., Creed, Cant., Deus
Mis.   Score **22**
     Short score **526**
     Organ part **1228**

Service in E mi. 4 v. *Boyce* (with Te D. instead of Bdte.). Bdte.,
Jub., Ky., Creed, Cant., and Deus Mis.   Score **1***
     Short score **526**

Jub., Cant., Deus Mis. Score (unfinished) **22**

Te Deum of same service. Score **22**

The same. Te D., Jub., Ky., Creed, instrumental parts (Vo. 1 and 2,
Bass) **1203**

Service in G. 3–4 v. *Boyce* (without Bdtus., Sctus., Glor., Cant., and
Deus Mis.). Te D., Bdtus., Jub., Ky., Creed, Sctus., Glor.,
‘Triple Commandments’ and ‘Triple Creed’ (i. e. in triple time),
Cant., D. Mis., Mag., and N. Dim. Score **780**

Single Chant. 4 v. *Boyce* **48**

Single Chant **1229**

ANTHEMS AND MOTETS.

And I heard a great voice. Score **621**
     Short score **525**

As on Euphrates. 3 v. Score **14**

Behold in heaven. See under *Aldrich*.

Christ being raised from the dead. Organ part **1233**

God is our hope. 8 v. *Boyce*. Organ part **1***
     Score **1205**

How art thou fallen. 2 v. *Harmonia Sacra*, Bk. I, 1688
     Score **14, 621**

How doth the city. 3 v. Score **14, 22**

I beheld and lo. V. A. *Harmonia Sacra*, Bk. II, 1714. *Boyce*.
     Score **782**
     Organ part **1229**

BLOW (John)—*continued.*

I said In the cutting off.   V. A. with instruments.
         Score   **621** wanting end, **628, 691**
I was in the Spirit.   V. A.   *Boyce*, &c.   Score   **16**
  (An adaptation, ? by Aldrich, of 'And I heard a great voice,' q.v.)
I will cry.   V. A.   Score   **14, 22**
Jesus seeing the multitude.   V. A.   Score   **14, 22**
Lord how are they increased.   V. A.   *Warren's Boyce*, &c.
         Score   **12, 22**
         Short score   **525**
My God my soul is vexed.   Sep. parts.   A. T. B. only   **1220–4**
         Organ parts   **1228, 1230**
O give thanks.   V. A. with instruments.   Score   **628**
O God wherefore art.   5 v.   *Boyce*.   Sep. parts.   A. T. B. only
                    1220–4
         Organ part   **1230**
O Lord I have sinned.   V. A.   *Boyce*.   Score   **14, 22**
Save me O God. V. A. *Boyce*. Sep. parts. A. T. B. only **1220–4**
         Organ part   **1230**
Sing we merrily.   V. A.   *Page*.   Score   **14**
         Sep. parts.   A. T. B. only   **1220–4**
         Organ part   **1229**
The kings of Tharsis.   V. A. with instruments.   Score   **628**
The Lord hear thee.   4 v.   Score   **48**
         Organ part   **1228**
The Lord is my shepherd.   V. A. with instruments.   Score   **628**
Turn thee unto me.   V. A.   Score   **14, 18, 22**
         Sep. parts.   S. A. B. only   **623–6**
When the Lord turned.   V. A. with instruments.   Score   **628**
When Israel came out of Egypt.   Organ part   **1233**
Cantate Domino.   2 v.   Score   **14**
Gloria Patri.   2 v.   Score   **14, 22**
Gloria Patri qui creavit nos.   5 v.   Score   **14**
In lectulo meo.   2 v.   Score   **14**
Laudate nomen.   2 v.   Score   **14**
Paratum cor meum.   2 v.   Score   **14**
Post hæc audivi.   2 v.   Score   **14**
Quam diligo legem.   2 v.   Score   **14**
Salvator mundi.   5 v.   Score   **14**

Songs, Cantatas, &c.

Arise my darken'd melancholy soul.   Tenor Solo   **350**
Awake my lyre. David's song to Michal, by Cowley. Sopr. Solo **49**
         The same for Sopr. Solo with 4 part Chos. and
            accompaniments for Vo. 1 and 2, and Bass.   Score **23**
Come poetry and with you bring.   Sopr. Solo and 3 part Chos.
         Score   **350**

BORRI (Giovanni Battista). 'Bolognese in Roma.' 17th century.

'Messa a 4 con V.V. e Rip°.' Kyrie eleison and Gloria in
 excelsis.   Sep. parts   1085–1108
                First Treble voice part only   529
                Single parts. 1st Treble voice, Vo. 1 (incomplete),
                 Vo. 2, Vcello   69, 70, 71, 73
 Credo a 5.   Sep. parts   1162–71

BOWMAN (Henry); published a volume of songs at Oxford
 in 1678.

Miserere mei Deus.   1–3 v.   Score   784
I'll sing of Heroes.   3 v. (T.T.B.) and Basso, from the Songs,
 1678.   Sep.   623–6

BOYCE (? Thomas, Mus. Bac. Oxon., 1603; or William, to whom
 are attributed some Fancies in R.C.M. Library, and who may
 be the William Boys, temporary organist of Lincoln, 1593.)

If ye love me.   4 v.   Short score   6

BOYCE (William).   1710–79.   Mus. Doc., Organist of the Chapel
 Royal.

I will alway give thanks.   Organ part   1233
Sing unto the Lord.   Organ part   1235
Single Chant in A   1229
Double Chant in B♭ (or by Cooke)   1226

BRODERIPP (   )

Single Chant in G mi.   1229

BRUNO (Guil.), a 17th-century organist.   See *Eitner*.

Toccata for the Organ   89

BRUSTERS, elsewhere spelt Brusser, and perhaps Brewster.   A
 16th-century writer.

In nomine in 5 parts   984–8

BRYNE (Albertus).   *c.* 1621–*c.* 1677.   Organist of St. Paul's, and
 later of Westminster Abbey.

Service in G.   4 v.   *Arnold.*   Te D., Jub., Ky., Creed, Mag.,
 N. Dim.   Score   1002
The same without Ky. and Creed.   Organ part   1225
                Sep. parts.   A. T. B. only   1220–4
Saraband and aire for Harpsichord   1177
Piece for Harpsichord   1236

BULL (John).   ? 1562–1628. Mus. Doc. Gentleman and Organist of
 the Chapel Royal.   Gresham Professor of Music, 1596.   Left
 England 1613.   Organist at Brussels and Antwerp, where he
 died.

BULL (John)—*continued.*
Almighty God which by the leading of a Star. V. A. for 2 Trebles
and Instruments and 5-part Chorus. Sep. parts wanting Bass
56–60

       Chorus parts, A. T. B. only   **1220–4**
       Organ part   **47**
The same. O Lord my God. *Boyce.* See under *Aldrich.*
How joyful and how glad. V. A. with Instruments and 5-part
Chorus. Sep. parts wanting Bass   **56–60**
In thee O Lord. 'For 2 meanes.' Organ part   **1001**
In nomine. 5 parts. Sep.   **984–8**
Prelude for the Virginal. From *Parthenia*   **431, 1179**
Eight Almaines, 2 Pavins, Dorick 3 pts., Dorick 4 pts., 2 Preludes,
Walsingham, Faire and Sweet, In nomine, Miserere, and 2
unnamed pieces for the Virginal   **1113**
Of these the Almaines No. 77 and 88 and 109 are also in   **1003**
       The Miserere is in   **1207**
    (Of the pieces contained in MS. 1113 the following are found
in the Fitzwilliam Virginal Book (edited by Maitland and Squire).
Almain No. 103 is in Vol II, p. 470; there anonymous and
called 'Dalling Alman'. The Prelude, No. 110 (a) is that in
Vol. II, p. 274. 'Walsingham' is in Vol. I, p. 1. The 'In
Nomine' is in Vol. II, p. 34. The 'Miserere', Vol. II, p. 442.
The unnamed piece No. 67 is that in Vol. I, p. 138.
    The 'Almain' No. 109 is a setting of 'Meridian Alman',
Vol. II, p. 477: there 'Set by Giles Farnaby'.)
'The Dutches of Brunswicks delight,' for the Virginal   **431**
    (Fitzwilliam V. Book, II, p. 146: there called 'The Duke of
Brunswick's Alman'.)

BYRD (William). *c.* 1542–1623. Organist of Lincoln, 1563.
Gentleman of the Chapel Royal, 1569.

SERVICES.

Short Service. *Barnard ; Boyce.* Te D., Bdtus., Ky., Creed, Mag.,
N. Dim. Sep. parts. A. T. T. B. only   **1220–4**
      Score, without words   **1002, 37**
      Short score, without words   **525**
      Organ parts   **437, 438, 1231**
      Organ part, without Bdtus., Ky., and Creed   **88**
      Organ part. The whole with Venite   **1001**
Evening service. *Barnard.* Mag. and N. Dim. 'For a Man
a lone.' Sep. parts. A. T. B. chorus parts only   **1220–4**
      Organ part   **1227**
Evening service. *Barnard.* Mag. and N. Dim. 'Mr. Birds
3 minnoms.' Organ part   **1001**

BYRD (William)—*continued.*
    ' Mr. Birds Answers.' Preces, suffrages, &c. Printed by *Jebb.*
        Treble and Bass only   **88**
        An incomplete copy of the same, scratched out, is in the
    same MS.

ANTHEMS.

Those marked * are printed in *Psalmes, Sonets and Songs, &c.,*
    1588.
Those marked † are printed in *Songs of sundrie natures, &c.,* 1589.
Arise O Lord why sleepest. Sep. A. T. B. only   **1220–4**
        Organ part   **1001**
Be not wroth. 5 v. See under *Aldrich.*
*Blessed is he. 5 v. Words in 2 Treble only   **984–8**
Bow thine ear. 5 v. Part II of O Lord, turn thy wrath. Adapted
    from Civitas sancti tui, q. v. *Barnard, Boyce.* Score   **1***
        Organ parts   **15, 47**
*Care for thy soul. 5 v. Words in 2 Treble only. Sep.   **984–8**
†Christ rising } 6 v. Sep. parts. A. T. T. B. chorus parts only
†Christ is risen }   **1220–4**
*Euen from the depth. 5 v. Words in 2 Treble only   **984–8**
Heare my prayer. *Barnard.* V. A. Sep. A. T. B. Chos. parts
    only   **1220–4**
        Organ parts   **6, 1001**
Howe long shall myne enemies. 5 v. Sep.   **984–8**
        Sep. A. T. B. only   **1220–4**
        Organ part   **1001**
*How shall a young man. 5 v. Words in 2 Treble only   **984–8**
*If that a sinners sighes. 5 v. Words in 2 Treble only   **984–8**
Let God arise. Bass part only   **1012**
*Lord in thy wrath. 5 v. Words in 2 Treble only   **984–8**
        Treble and Bass   **439**
My faltes O Christ. 5 v. Words in Treble only   **984–8**
*My soule opprest. Treble and Bass only   **439**
O God the proud. V. A. 6 v. Sep. parts. T. (V. and Chos.).
    A. and B. (Chos.) parts only   **1220–4**
        Organ part   **1001**
O God whom our offences. *Barnard.* Organ part.   **1001**
O Lorde howe vaine (Vpon Sr Philip Sidneis dittie). 5 v. Words
    in 1 Treble only. Sep.   **984–8**
O Lord how longe. Treble and Bass   **439**
O Lord make thy servant (Elizabeth, King Charles, &c., with name
    altered for different reigns). 5 v. *Barnard.* Sep. parts   **984–8**
        T. and B. parts only   **1220–4**
        Short score   **525**
        Organ parts   **47, 1001**
        Organ part (ascribed to ' Cranford ')   **1230**
        For 6 v. (adapted by ? Aldrich). Score   **16** (twice), **37**

BYRD (William)—*continued*.

 O Lord within thy tabernacle. 5 v. Words in 2 Treble only
                   984–8

 O Lord turn thy wrath. Pt. I. 5 v. Adapted from Ne irascaris,
  q. v. *Barnard, Boyce.* Score   1*
    Organ part   47
 Prevent us O Lorde. 5 v. *Barnard.* Sep.   984–8
    Bass only   1012
    Organ part   1001
 *Prostrate O Lorde. 5 v. Words in 1 Treble only. Sep. 984–8
 Save me O God. Warren's *Boyce.* Sep. parts wanting Bass
                 56–60
    Score   16
    Bass voice only   1012
    Organ parts   1001, 1230
 Sing joyfully. 6 v. *Barnard, Boyce.* Score (two copies) 16
    Sep. parts, A. T. B. only   1220–4
    Short score   525
    Organ parts   47, 1001, 1230
 Teach me O Lorde. V. A. 5 v. *Barnard* (3rd Ps., 2nd Preces,
  &c.). Organ part   6
 Thou God that guidest. V. A. 5 v. *Barnard.* Organ parts 6, 1001
 Triumph with pleasant melodie. 5 v. Words in 1 Treble only.
  Sep.   984–8
 What unacqueinted cheerful voice. 5 v. Words in 1 Treble only.
  Sep.   984–8

MOTETS, &c.

Those marked * are printed in *Liber Primus Sacrarum Cantionum,*
 1589.

Those marked † are printed in *Liber Secundus Sacrarum Cantionum,* 1591.

N.B.—All those contained in the MSS. 979–83 are imperfect, as
 the Tenor Book is wanting in this set.

†Afflicti pro peccatis, with 2nd part, Et eruas. 6 v. Sep. 979–83
Alleluja confitemini. 3 v.   45
†Apparebit in finem. 5 v. Sep.   979–83, 984–8
*Aspice domine de sede, with 2nd part, Respice domine. 5 v.
 Sep.   979–83
Audivi vocem. 5 v. Sep.   979–83, 984–8
Benigne fac. 5 v. Sep.   979–83
†Circumdederunt me. 5 v. Sep.   979–83
*Civitas sancti tui. Pt. II of Ne irascaris, q. v. 5 v. Sep. 984–8
    Score   10
†Cunctis diebus. 6 v. Sep.   979–83
De Lamentatione : Beth, Cogitavit : Teth, Defixæ : Joth, Sederunt :
 and Jerusalem convertere. 5 v. Sep.   979–83
†Descendit de celis, with 2nd part, Et exivit. 6 v. Sep. 979–83

c

BYRD (William)—*continued.*

Deus in adiutorium. 6 v. Sep.   979–83
*Deus venerunt, with 2nd part, Posuerunt. 5 v. Sep.   984–8
Domine ante te. 6 v. Sep.   979–83
Domine Deus omnipotens. 5 v. Sep.   979–83
†Domine exaudi, with 2nd part, Et non intres. 5 v. Sep.
                                                 979–83, 984–8
*Domine præstolamur, with 2nd part, Veni Domine. 5 v. Sep.
                                                 979–83, 984–8
*Domine tu jurasti. 5 v. Sep.   984–8
*Effuderunt sanguinem. Pt. III of Deus venerunt. 5 v. Sep.
                                                            984–8
†Exurge Domine. 5 v. Sep.   979–83, 984–8
†Fac cum servo. 5 v. Sep.   984–8
*Facti sumus opprobrium. Pt. IV of Deus venerunt. 5 v. Sep.
                                                            984–8
*In resurrectione. 5 v. Sep.   984–8
†Infelix ego, with 2nd and 3rd parts, Quid igitur and Ad te igitur.
    6 v. Sep.   979–83
            Triplex and Medius and Tenor of opening passage
            only   45
*Lætentur cœli, with 2nd part, Orietur. 5 v. Sep.   984–8
†Levemus corda. 5 v. Sep.   979–83
*Memento Domine. 5 v. Sep.   979–83
†Miserere mei. 5 v. Sep.   984–8
*Ne irascaris. Pt. I   979–83, 984–8
            Score   10
Ne perdas. 5 v. Sep.   979–83
Noctis recolitur. 5 v. Sep.   979–83
Non nobis Domine. Canon (without composer's name)   89
*O Domine adjuva. 5 v. Sep.   979–83, 984–8
*O quam gloriosum, with 2nd part, Benedictio et claritas. 5 v.
    Sep.   979–83, 984–8
O salutaris. 6 v. Sep.   979–83
Omni tempore. 5 v. Sep.   979–83
Peccavi super numerum. 5 v. Sep.   979–83
Precamur sancte. 5 v. Sep.   984–8
Reges Tharsis. 5 v. Sep.   979–83
Sanctus, sanctus, sanctus. 3 v.   45
†Tribulatio proxima, with 2nd part, Contumelias et terrores. 5 v.
    Sep.   984–8
†Tribulationes civitatis, with 2nd and 3rd parts, Timor et hebetudo
    and Nos enim. 5 v. Sep.   979–83, 984–8
†Tristitia et anxietas, with 2nd part, Sed tu Domine. 5 v. Sep.
                                                 979–83, 984–8
†Vide Domine, with 2nd part, Sed veni Domine. 5 v. Sep.
                                                         979–83

BYRD (William)—*continued.*

MADRIGALS, SONGS, &C.

Those marked * are printed in *Psalmes, Sonets, and songs,* &c., 1588.
Those marked † are printed in *Songs of sundrie natures,* &c., 1589.

Blame I confes.   5 v.   Words in 1 Treble only.   Sep.   **984–8**
*Come to me grief.   Funeral song of Sir Philip Sidney.   5 v.
   Words in 1 Treble only.   Sep.   **984–8**
*Constante Penelope.   5 v.   Treble and Bass only   **439**
*I ioy not.   Words in 1 Treble only.   5 v.   Sep.   **984–8**
*If wemen could.   5 v.   Words in 1 Treble only.   Sep.   **984–8**
*In fields abrode.   5 v.   Words in 1 Treble only.   Sep.   **984–8**
   Treble and Bass only   **439**
*La Verginella.   5 v.   Words in 1 Treble only.   Sep.   **984–8**
*Lullaby, with 2nd part, Be still.   5 v.   Words in 2 Treble only.
   Sep. parts   **984–8**
   Treble and Bass parts only   **439**
*My mynde to me.   5 v.   Words in 1 Treble only.   Sep.   **984–8**
   Treble and Bass only   **439**
My little sweet darling.   5 v.   Words in Treble only.   Cf. B. M.
   Add. MSS. 17786, &c.   Sep. parts   **984–8**
Oh golden heares.   5 v.   Words in 1 Treble only.   Sep.   **984–8**
*O that most rare.   A funeral song upon Sir Philip Sidney ; with
   2nd part, For thee both kings ; and 3rd part, The doleful debt.
   5 v.   Words in 1 Treble only.   Sep.   **984–8**
*Susanna faire.   5 v.   Words in 1 Treble only.   Sep.   **984–8**
The daie delaied.   a 5.   (Cf. B. M. Add. MS. 31992.)   Sep. parts.
   984–8
*Though Amaryllis.   5 v.   Words in 1 Treble only.   Sep.   **984–8**
   Treble and Bass only   **439**
†When I was otherwise.   5 v.   Words in 1 Treble only.   Sep.   **984–8**
*Where fancie fond.   5 v.   Words in 1 Treble only.   Sep.   **984–8**
While Phebus.   5 v.   Words in 1 Treble only.   Sep.   **984–8**
*Who likes to love.   5 v.   Words in 1 Treble only.   Sep.   **984–8**
*Why do I use.   5 v.   Words in 2 Treble only.   Sep.   **984–8**

INSTRUMENTAL MUSIC.

Browning.   5 parts.   Sep.   **984–8**
In nomine.   5 parts.   Sep.   **984–8**
A songe of tow bases.   6 parts.   Sep.   Wanting Tenor book
   979–83

Miserere for organ   **371**
Galliard (*sic*) for Virginal   **1175**
If my complaintes.   Variations on a song by Dowland (q.v.) for
   Virginal   **431**
Fantasia for Virginal (*Fitzwilliam Virginal Book,* vol. ii, p. 406)
   1113
' Mr. Birds battle ' for Virginal   **431**
   The movements are headed :—' The souldiers sum̃uns.   The

C 2

BYRD (William)—*continued.*

marche of the foote men. The march of the horse men. The Trumpetts. The Irish march. The bagpipe and the drume (two movements). The second change. The third. The fourth change. The fifte chaunge. The last chaunge. The march to the fight.' Unfinished.

C. (S.).

A piece for Harpsichord called The Countess of Portland's Delight.
92

Arise, shine, for thy light.   Bass only   366
O God wherefore art thou absent.   2 v.   Bass only   366
Turn in my Lord, turn in to me.   2 v.   Treble and Bass   365
        Bass only   366

C. (T.).

Fantazia a 4. Sep.   423–8

CALDERI (Agostino) : a 17th-century writer.

Chi non sà che sia l'amare.   Aria for Sopr. Solo   954
Per far certa.   Aria for Sopr. Solo   954
Resisto mà in vano.   Aria for Sopr. Solo   954

CALISTA (Lelio).   A 17th-century writer, one of whose Sonatas is quoted by Purcell in his edition of Playford's *Introduction to the Skill of Musik*, 1694.   (See Mr. Barclay Squire, *Internat. Musikgesellschaft, Sammelbände* 1904–5, p. 557.)

Bass parts of Sonatas, numbered *prima* to *sesta*   1126
Sonata in B♭.   Two movements.   2 Trebles and Basso continuo.
        Score   1126
Sonata 11th in G.   Two Trebles and Basso cont.   1126
Extracts from Sonatas in various keys   1126
    (Other Sonatas in this MS. may also be by Calista.)

CAMPION (Thomas).   1567–1620.

Com you prettie false eyd wanton.   Treble and Bass.   From *The Second Book of Ayres*   87
Thoughe you are younge.   Treble voice with Bass : from Rosseter's *A Booke of Ayres*, 1601   439

CAREY (Henry).   *c.* 1690–1743.

I'll range around.   Treble Solo   1215
    [Engraved about 1720.]

CARISSIMI (Giacomo) 1604–74.   Chapel master of S. Apollinare, Rome.

For Anthems adapted by Aldrich from Carissimi's works, see under *Aldrich.*

CARISSIMI (Giacomo)—*continued.*

MASSES, &C.

Mass in C.   3 v.   T. T. B.   Score   **23, 55**
The same, somewhat altered, with 1 and 2 Violin parts.   Score **13**
Mass in C.   5 v. with verses.   (Without name, but stated on the
   binding to be by Carissimi.)   **49**
Jephta: an oratorio.   Score   **37**
          Plorate filiae Israel.   6 v. from *Jephta*.   Score   **13**
Judicium Salomonis.   'A solis ortu.'   1–4 v.   S. S. T. B.
   Score   **53**
The same with Violin parts, 'The symphonies being not Caris-
   simi's but some musty Dutchman's.'   Score   **13**

MOTETS.

The Motets marked with an asterisk are printed in *Sacri Concerti*,
   1675.   Those with a dagger in Floridus de Sylvestris's *Cantiones
   Sacræ*, 1657 and 1663.
Anima mea in æterna dulcedine.   2 v.   S. B.
      Score   **43, 621, 1178**
      Sep. parts   **623–6**
Anima nostra.   2 v.   S. S.   Score   **55**
*Annunciate gentes.   1–5 v.   Score   **13, 53**
Audite sancti.   3 v.   S. S. B.   Playford's *Harmonia Sacra*, Bk. II,
   1693.   Score   **43, 53**
      Sep. parts   **623–6**
Ave dulcissime.   3 v.   S. S. T.   Score   **13**
Benedicite omnes angeli.   3 v.   A. T. B.   Score   **13**
*Cantabo Domino.   2 v.   S. S.   Score   **13, 53**
Confitebor tibi.   3 v.   S. S. B.   Score   **13**
[? Crucior in hac flamma.   2 v.   A. B.   Dialogue Angelus et
   Anima, here called *Italica comp* : ascribed to Carissimi in Fitz-
   william Mus. Cambridge Catalogue   **1154]**
*Cum ingrederetur N. in paradisi gloriam.   3 v.   S. S. S.
      Score   **53**
*The same, with words Cum reverteretur David.   Score   **13**
*Dicite nobis.   4 v.   S. S. A. T.   Score   **13, 53**
Dixit Dominus.   1–5 v.   Score   **55**
†Domine Deus meus.   S. Solo   **13, 53**
*Domine quis habitabit.   3 v.   S. S. T.   Score   **13, 53**
Ego sum panis.   3 v.   S. S. B.   Sep. parts   **688**
Egredimini cælestis.   3 v.   S. S. S.   Score   **13, 53**
Exultabunt justi.   3 v.   S. S. S.   Score   **13, 53**
*Exulta, gaude filia.   2 v.   S. S.   Score   **13**
The same without the 'Noe' at end   **53**
Gaudete exercitus.   3 v.   S. S. B.   **13, 53**
Hodie Simon Petrus.   2 v.   T. T.   Score   **13, 53**

CARISSIMI (Giacomo)—*continued.*

In te Domine. 3 v. A. T. B. with instruments. Score	4
Gloria Patri from the same. Score	53
*Laudemus virum. 2 v. S. S. Score	13, 53
Lucifer cælestis. Bass Solo. Playford's *Harmonia Sacra*, Bk. II, 1693	18, 23, 53
The same, transposed for Soprano. Voice part only	598
Militia est vita. 3 v. S. S. B. Score	13, 53
Non turbetur cor. 2 v. S. B. Sep.	688
O dulcissimum Mariæ. 2 v. S. S. Score	13
O quam mirabilia. 2 v. S. S. Score	55
O quam suave. 3 v. S. S. S. Score	83
O vulnera doloris. 3 v. S. S. B. Score	13
The same for Bass voice and Basso only	46, 53
Basso only	1210
Basso only unfinished	13
Pastores dum custoditis. Sopr. Solo	13
†Prævaluerunt in nos. 3 v. S. A. T. Also in P. Phalese's *Florida Verba*, Antwerp, 1661. Score	13
Quid agis cor. Sopr. Solo	13
Quis est hic. 3 v. S. S. S. Score	13, 53
*Quo tam lætus. 2 v. S. S. Score	13, 53
Quomodo facti sunt. 3 v. S. S. B. Score	13
Sicut erat in principio. Instr. Bass only	75
Sicut mater. 2 v. S. S. Score	55
Sicut stella. Sopr. Solo	13 unfinished, 53
Surgamus eamus. 3 v. A. T. B. Score	13, 53
Suscitavit Dominus. 3 v. A. T. B. Score	13
*Turbabuntur impii. 3 v. A. T. B. Score	13, 53
Venite pastores. Sopr. Solo.	13
†Vidi impium. 3 v. A. T. B. Score	13

CANTATAS, &c.

A piè d'un verde: 'Democritus et Heraclitus'. 2 v. S. S. Score	52
Alma che fai. 2 v. S. B. Score	52, 996
Almeno un pensiero. Sopr. Solo	949, 51
Amanti sentite. 2 v. S. A.	18
The same, without composer's name. Score	350
Sep. parts	623–6
Alto voice only	49
The same, attributed to Sigr. Marco. (See *Cesti*)	996
Ardeua in tanto. Sopr. Solo	51
Ardo lassa. Sopr. solo	998, 51 unfinished
Bel tempo per me. Sopr. Solo	949, 51
Care selve beate. Bass Solo	18, 1215
Unfinished	13

CARISSIMI (Giacomo)—*continued.*
Vaghi rai pupille. 2 v. S. S.	**996, 54**
Va, va, dimanda. Sopr. Solo	**51**
Vittoria, vittoria	**17, 350**
Short extracts without words. T. B. B.	**1124**

CARLO DEL VIOLINO, a 17th-century Italian composer.
Non si tema, ' La Regina de Tunesi '. Sopr. Solo	**998**
Pur che lo sappi. 2 v. S. S. (here attributed to *Rossi*, but see *Wotquenne*)	**996**
Rido una uolta. Sopr. Solo	**952, 956**

CARWARDEN (John).   Contributed to Playford's *Court Ayres*, 1655. A portrait of Christopher Simpson painted by him is in the Music School Collection.   See *Musical Antiquary*, April 1913.
Prelude, Almaine, &c. Seven pieces in 2 parts for instruments, of which the first and last have the composer's name. Treble and Bass. Sep. parts	**1006–9**
Eighteen Almains, Corants, &c. Bass only	**1011**

CASATI (Gasparo).   Chapel master at Novara, 1641.

Motets from *Moteta una et duabus vocibus ad Organum concertata* : a copy of the Antwerp edition, 1662, is in this Library.
Bone Jesu. 2 v. S. or T. Scores	**20, 621**
Sep. parts	**623–6**
Magnificate cæli. 2 v. S. or T. Sep.	**623–6**
O dulce nomen. 2 v. S. or T. Scores	**20, 621**
Sep. parts	**623–6**
O Jesu mea vita. 2 v. T. T. Sep.	**623–6**
One T. part only	**1173**
Omnes gentes. 2 v. S. or T. Sep.	**623–6**
Regina cæli. 2 v. S. or T. Sep.	**623–6**
One S. part only	**1173**
Tota pulchra es. 2 v. S. or T. Scores	**20, 621**
Sep.	**623–6**

CASTRO (Jean de).   Born at Évreux ; fl. 1571–96.
Tell me thou man. Canzonet for 3 v. (2 copies of Sopr. 1 and 2). Sep.	**739–43**

CAVENDISH (Michael), fl. 1592–1601.
Every bush new springinge. (Ascribed to Cavendish in B. M. Add. MS. 31811.) Treble voice with Bass	**439**

CECCHELLI (Carlo), fl. 1645–64.   Chapel master at Rome and at Loretto.
Dicite laudem. Motet a 3. A. T. B. Score	**14**

CESTI (Marc' Antonio), *c.* 1620–69. Chapel master at Florence, 1646; member of the Papal Choir, 1660; Vice-chapelmaster at Vienna, 1666.

Motets.

Filiæ Jerusalem. 4 v. S. S. S. B. Score	83
Maria et flumina. 2 v. S. S. Score	83
Properate mortales. Sopr. Solo	83

Cantatas, &c., all for Sopr. Solo.

Bella Clori	83
Cara e dolce libertà. Printed in Pignani's *Scelta di Canzonette*, London, 1679, as by Cesti. A version for 2 voices printed by Hawkins (iv, 94) 1776, as by Cesti. Printed as by A. Scarlatti in Thirty-six Ariettas, London, *c.* 1753	958
Del famoso Oriente, 'La Madre Ebrea'	83
Del ricercar qual sorte	83
Due begl' occhi	948
Esser colpa come	947
Ferma Lachesi	83
Gia il sonno	949
Insegnatemi à morire	83
[L]anguia gia l'alba	83
Lasciatemi	83
Mancauano tormenti	949
Partiteui respiri	83
Quanto sete	83
Quanto è dolce	947
Solingo un di Fileno	83
Vi conosco luci	948
Voi colpate	948

The following by 'Sig^r. Marco' and 'Sig^r. Marc'Antonio' may be assigned to Cesti.

All' assedio. 3 v. S. S. A. 'Sig^r. Marco'	996
Amanti sentite. 2 v. S. A. 'Sig^r. Marco'	996
The same, attributed to *Carissimi*, q. v.	18
The same, without composer's name. Scores	350, 377
Sep. parts	623–6
Alto voice only	49
Gia son morto. 2 v. S. S. 'S. Marc'Antonio'	996
Without composer's name	377

CHAMBONNIÈRES (Jacques Champion de). First Harpsichord player to Louis XIV; published 2 volumes of Harpsichord Music in 1670. The following piece is ascribed to 'Sambonier', by which name Chambonnières seems to be intended.

Corant for Harpsichord	1236

CHARD (   ). Probably George William, Mus.D., Organist of
    Winchester Cathedral, 1802–49.
    Three Chants   **1226**

CHILD (William). ? 1606–97. Mus. Doc. Organist of St. George's,
    Windsor.
    Evening Service in C mi. ' Flat service for verses.' Mag. and N.
      Dim. Sep. A. T. B. only   **1220–4**
          Mag. unfinished. S. and B. parts only without words **22**
          Organ part   **1227**
    ' Sharpe Service ' in D. 4 v. *Boyce.* Te D., Jub., Ky., Creed, Mag.,
      N. Dim. Sep. parts. A. T. B. only.   **1220–4**
          Short score   **525**
          Score   **1002**
          Without Ky. and Creed. Organ part   **1227**
    Kyrie and Creed to Morley's service ; in D mi. Sep. parts. A. T. B.
      only   **1220–4**
    Service in E mi. 4 v. *Boyce.* Te D., Jub., Ky., Creed, Mag.,
      N. Dim. Score   **1002**
          Short score   **525**
          Bass part only   **1012**
          Mag. and N. Dim. only. Tenor part   **440**
    Service in E ♭. *Arnold.* Te D., Jub., Mag., N. Dim. Organ
      part   **1231**
    Service in F. 4 v. Te D., Jub., Ky., Creed, Cant., D. Mis.
          Score   **1002**
          Bass part only   **1012**
          Cant. and D. Mis. only. Short Score   **525**
    ' Second Service ' in G. 4 v. Bdte., Jub., Ky., Creed, Mag., N. Dim.
          Score   **1002**
          With Venite (T. and B. only): Offertorie ' Charge
            them ', Gloria, 8 v. (A. T. T. B. B. only.) Sep.
            A. T. B. only   **1220–4**
          Mag. and N. Dim. only. Organ parts   **1225, 1228**
          The same Jub. with Te Deum. Organ part   **1233**
          Cantate and D. Mis. in G. 4–5 v. Score   **1002**
    [These appear to be all parts of the same service.]
    Service, ' Full,' in A mi. *Ouseley.* Te D., Jub., Mag., N. Dim.
          Organ part   **1227**
    Evening Service, ' Verse,' in A mi. Mag. and N. Dim.
          Bass voice only   **1012**
          Organ part   **1227**

Anthems, &c.

Behold how good. V. A. Score   **12, 1002**
          Sep. parts   **623–6**
          Bass Chorus part only   **1012**

CHILD (William)—*continued*.
    If the Lord himselfe. 4 v. *Arnold*.
             Sep. parts, A. T. B. B. only   **1220–4**
             1 Bass only   **1012**
    Lord who shall dwell. V. A. Sep. A. T. B. only   **1220–4**
    O Lord God the heathen. F. A. Sep. A. T. B. only   **1220–4**
    O Lord grant the king. 4 v. With 5-part *Hallelujah*. *Boyce*.
             Sep. A. T. B. B. only   **1220–4**
             Bass part only   **1012**
             Organ part   **1228**
    O pray for the peace. 4 v. *Arnold*. Score   **1002**
             Short score   **525**
             Bass part only   **1012**
    Praise the Lord O my soule. 4 v. With the same *Hallelujah* as
    in 'O Lord grant the king'. *Boyce*. Score   **11**
             Sep. parts, A. T. B. B. only   **1220–4**
             Organ parts   **438, 1230**
    Sing we merrily. F. A. 7 v. *Boyce*. Sep. A. T. B. B. only **1220–4**
    Thou art my king. V. A. Score   **12**
             Sep. A. T. B. Chos. and B. verse only   **1220–4**
    Turn thou us. V. A. Sep. parts, A. T. T. B. B. only   **1220–4**
    Ye sons of Sion. A Christmas hymn. 2 v. S. and B.   **365**
    O bone Jesu. 4 v. S. A. T. B. Score   **14**
    Come Hymen come. A nuptial song. 3 v. A. T. B. Sep.
                        747–9

CHURCH (John), 1675–1741. Gent. of the Chapel Royal, 1697;
    Master of the Choristers, Westminster Abbey.

Service in F. 4 v. *Ouseley*. Te D., Jub., Ky., Creed, Mag.,
N. Dim. Score   **627**
Single chant in C mi.   **1226**

CLARKE (Jeremiah), *c.* 1669–1707. Master of the Choristers at
    St. Paul's, 1693; Gent. of the Chapel Royal, 1700; Joint
    Organist of the Chapel Royal, 1704.

How long. *Boyce*. Organ part   **1234**
             Chorus only to 'How long'. Organ parts **1228, 1235**
I will exalt thee. Organ part   **1229**
I will love thee. *Boyce*. Score incomplete   **1111**
I will love thee. A thanksgiving anthem. V. A. for A. T. B.,
    4-part Chorus and Organ   **48**
The Lord is my strength. *Page*. 'A thanksgiving anthem,
    June 27, 1706.' V. A. for A. T. B., 4-part Chorus and Organ.
             Score   **48**
O Lord God of my salvation. *Page*. Organ part   **1226**
Praise the Lord O Jerusalem. *Boyce*. Organ part   **1228**

CLARKE (Jeremiah)—*continued.*
The Lord is full of compassion.   *Cathedral Mag.*   Organ part
1235
'All for the better.'   Overture, Gavott, Hornpipe Round O, Aire,
Aire, Round O, Farewell, Aire, Minuet Round O, from Manning's
'All for the better,' 1702.   4 parts in Score   **3**
The 'Round O', Treble and Bass only   **620**
Air and Serenade for Harpsichord: both printed in *A Choice
Collection of Ayres*, 1700   **46**

CLARKE (John), afterwards Clarke-Whitfeld.   Mus. Doc.   Organist
of Armagh, 1794–7; Professor of Music in the University of
Cambridge.   Died 1836.
Six Chants   **1226**

COBB (John).   Gent. of the Chapel Royal, 1638.   Contributed to
Lawes's *Choice Psalmes*, 1648, when he is called 'Organist of
his Majesties Chappell Royall'.
Two Almaines and two Corants in 3 parts.   Sep. parts   **379–81**

COLEMAN (Charles).   Mus. Doc.   Chamber musician to James I;
Musician for Lute and Voices to Charles I; Musician for Viol,
1660, and Composer in his Majesty's Private Music for Voices,
1662.   Died 1664.
Nine Almaines in 3 parts.   Sep.   **379–81**
Five Almaines, four Corantos, and 'A Northern Saraband' in
3 parts, by C. C. (probably Coleman).   Sep.   **379–81**
(Other compositions in these MSS. are probably by Coleman.)
Six Almaines in 4 parts.   Sep.   **367–70**
Fantazia in 5 parts.   For Organ   **1004**
The same.   Sep. parts for instruments   **423–8, 473–8**
Five fancies in 6 parts.   Sep. parts   **61–6**
The 2nd and 5th of these   **473–8**
The 1st, 2nd, and 5th of these.   Sep., **403–8**; In Score, **2**;
Short Score, **436**.
Three Ayres, three Corantes, one Pavin, one Saraband for instru-
ments.   Treble only   **1022**
Aire, Corant, Saraband; 'Eccho Almaine, Eccho Corranto, Eccho
Sarabrand'; Aire, Coranto, Saraband (3 sets); Almaine, Coranto,
Saraband (3 sets).   Bass part only   **1011**
Piece for instruments in 3 parts, with Basso.   Sep.   **353–6**
(The name Coleman is here prefixed to the first (only) of 45
pieces, probably all his.)

COLEMAN (Mark).   A 17th-century writer.
Corant for Harpsichord   **1236**

COOKE (Henry). Master of the Children of the Chapel Royal, 1660. Died 1672.

Turn thou us.   V. A.   Score   12, 14, 22
              Verse part.   Treble voice only   598
Awake my soule.   The morning hymn.   Sopr. Solo   49
Sleepe downy sleepe.   The evening hymn.   Sopr. Solo   49, 1205
         (Cf. B. M. Add. MS. 33234.)
As on a river's side.   Sopr. Solo   49

COPERARIO or **COPRARIO (John)**, properly Cooper. Chamber Musician to Charles I. Died 1627.

Six songs from *Songs of Mourning : bewailing the vntimely death of Prince Henry*, 1613.   Bass voice only   366

O griefe how diuers.	Soe parted you.
Tis now dead night.	How like a golden dreame.
Fortune and glory.	When pale famine.

Instrumental music for Strings and Organ :
Fourteen Sets of 3 pieces (Fantazia, Alman and Ayre) for 1 Violin, Bass and Organ (numbered 41–82).   Sep.   **411–13**
The same.   Violin and Bass only   **732 and 4**
From the same, those numbered 59 to 71 with 61 and 64 interchanged.   Organ part   **15**
From the same.   The piece numbered 59.   Organ part, unfinished   **422**
Eight Sets of 3 pieces (Fantazia, Alman and Galliard) for 2 Violins, Bass and Organ.   Sep. parts without Organ part
               414–16, 732–4
Fantazias from Sets 5, 6, 7, 1, 2, and 3 of the same.   Violin parts only   **421**
Almans and Galliards from Sets 1, 2, 3 (No. 3 having a different Galliard), and 5.   Violin parts only   **421**

Instrumental pieces in 3 parts :
Seven fancies.   Sep. parts, wanting 1 Treble   **401–2**
         Score   **2**
The 2nd, 3rd, and 6th of the same   **473–8**
Two fancies not in **401–2**   **473–8**

Instrumental pieces in 4 parts :
Six Fancies.   Sep.   **423–8**
The first five of the same.   Sep.   **397–400**
         Score   **2**
         Short score   **436**
         Of these the 1st is sep.   **473–8**
One Fancy (not in above) sep.   **397–400, 473–8**
         Score   **2**
         Short score   **436**

COPERARIO or COPRARIO (John)—*continued*.

Instrumental pieces in 5 parts:

Eighteen pieces, 5 of which are named 'Deh cara', 'Corsea', 'Lucretia mia', 'Rapiua', 'Io piango'. Sep.   **527–30, 1024**

Of these, Nos. 11, 12, 13, 14, 24, 26, 27, 28, 29, 30, 31, 32, 34, 35, 36, 37 are sep.   **404–8**

 Short score   **436**

  The same except 13 and the opening of 11. Score   **2**

Nos. 12, 14, 30, 31, 32.   Score   **21**

Nos. 11 (Cresce in voi), 12, 25 (Fuga dunque la luce), 26 (O sonno), 27 (Luci beate), 33 (Voi caro), 34 (in 527–30 Corsea, called in 61–6 Crudel perche), 35 (Lucretia mia) are sep.   **61–6**

Nos. 24 and 37 (Io piango) are score   **44**

No. 14.   Organ parts   **67, 1004**

No. 32.   Organ part   **1004**

No. 11 (Cresce in voi) and 24.   Sep.   **423–8**

Three pieces called 'Leno', 'Io son ferito', 'Dolce ben mio'.

 Sep.   **61–6**

The 2 former of these.   Sep.   **404–8**

 Short score   **436**

'Io son ferito.'   Score   **2**

Two pieces, 'Fuggi' and 'Per far vna'.   Score   **44**

 Score   **2**

 Sep. parts   **404–8**

 Short score   **436**

'Fuggi.'   Score   **21**

Instrumental pieces in 6 parts.

Three fancies.   Sep.   **423–8**

The same for Organ   **1004**

Of these, No. 20.   Sep.   **404–8**

 Score   **2**

Fancy.   Sep.   **61–6**

CORELLI (Arcangelo), 1653–1713.   Born at Fusignano.   Died at Rome.

Sonata in B♭.   Vo. 1 and 2, Bass, and Basso continuo.   Sonata III, Opera terza.   Score   **620**

Gavotte from Sonata X, Opera quarta.   Vo. 1 only   **1111**

Gavotte from Sonata I, Opera seconda.   Vo. 1 only   **1111**

CORKINE (William), fl. 1610–12.

Prayse the Lord.   F. A. for 5 v., wanting Bass   **56–60**

CORMACK or CORMAKE (   ).   Perhaps Cormac MacDermot, Harper to Q. Elizabeth and James I.

Sir John Paiton's Pauan.   3 parts.   Sep.   **379–81**

Almaine.   Bass only   **1022**

CORNET (Pietro).   Organist at Brussels ; fl. 1624.
   Two Fantasias for Organ (one has initials P. C. only)   **89**

CORREGGIO (Claudio da).   See under *Merulo*.

CORSI (Giuseppe).   Chapel master at Rome, S. Maria Maggiore,
   1659 ; S. Giovanni in Laterano, 1663.
   Voglio amar chi piace.   Cantata for Sopr. Solo   **948**

COSYN (Benjamin).   Organist of Dulwich College, 1622–4, and of
   the Charterhouse, 1626–*c.* 1643 (*Musical Times*, Dec., 1903).
   He is known as the owner of a Virginal Book containing com-
   positions by him, now in the Buckingham Palace Library.
   O praise God in his holiness.   Anthem in 5 parts, without words.
         Score   **44**
   Eight pieces for Virginal, signed B. C.   **1113**
   (These may very probably be by Cosyn.)

COURTEVILLE (   ), probably Raphael or Ralph.   Organist
   of St. James's, Westminster.   Died *c.* 1735.
   Overture and 6 pieces for Strings.   Tenor and Bass only   **351–2**

CRANFORD or CRANFORTHE (William).   Contributed to Ravens-
   croft's Psalter, 1622.   Clifford, 1663, prints words of Anthems
   by him.
   My sinfull soule.   V. A. for 6 v.   Bass wanting   **56–60**
   Weepe, Brittaynes, weepe.   A passion on the death of Prince Henry.
   6 v.   Bass wanting   **56–60**
   Woods, rockes, and Mountaynes.   Madrigal for 6 v.   Bass wanting
         56–60
   In nomine a 5 for Instruments.   **423–8**
   Almaine in 3 parts.   Sep.   **379–81**

CREYGHTON (Robert), *c.* 1639–1734.   D.D.   Professor of Greek
   at Cambridge, 1662 ; Canon and Precentor of Wells, 1674.
   Service in B♭.   4 v.   Te D., Jub., Sctus., Ky., Creed, Mag., N. Dim.
         Sep. parts for voices and Organ.   **760**
   Service in E♭.   4 v.   *Boyce.*   Te D., Jub., Mag., N. Dim.
         Score   **40**
         Organ parts   **1229, 1232**
   Sanctus in F 'to King in F'.   Organ part   **1225**
   I will arise.   Anthem.   4 v.   *Boyce.*
         Sep. parts for voices and organ   **760**
         Organ part   **1228**

CROCE (Giovanni).   *c.* 1557–1609.   Chapel master of St. Mark's,
   Venice, 1603.   A collection of his sacred music with English
   words was published in London in 1608, under the name of
   Musica Sacra.

CROCE (Giovanni)—*continued.*

Lord in mercy remember. 3 v. S. S. A. Sep. parts, with 2 copies of 1 and 2 Treble   **739–43**

Lord in thine Anger, Pt. I.   6 v.
My strength euen fayles, Pt. II.   6 v. } from *Musica Sacra*, 1608.

     Organ part   **67**

Shew mercye, Pt. I.   6 v.
Give me a cleane heart, Pt. II.   6 v. } from *Musica Sacra*, 1608.

     Organ part   **67**

Sinne like a cunninge lurcher. Canzonet. 4 v. An adaptation to English words of 'La venenosa vista' in Croce's 4-part *Canzonette*, Venice, 1588. Sep. parts   **750–3**

View my harty contrytione. 4 v. Sep.   **750–3**

Cinthia thy song. Madrigal for 5 v. from Yonge's *Musica Transalpina*, Book II, 1597. Score   **33**

CROFT (William). 1678–1727. Mus. Doc. Gentleman extraordinary of the Chapel Royal, 1700, and Joint Organist, 1704; Organist, 1707; Organist of Westminster Abbey, 1708.

(The works marked with an asterisk were printed in his *Musica Sacra*, 1724.)

Service in E♭. 3–6 v. Te D., Jub., Cant., Deus Mis. Score **40**

     Organ part, Te D. and Jub. **1232**; Cant. and D. Mis.   **1233**

Morning Service in A. 4 v. Te D., Jub., Ky., Creed. Score **40**

     Organ part   **1232**

     Kyrie only, Organ part   **1225**

Morning Service in B mi. 4–6 v. Te D. and Jub. *Arnold*

     Score   **23, 40**

*Burial Service. Treble voice only   **69**

ANTHEMS.

*Blessed are all they. Organ part   **1234**

Blessed is the people. Playford's *Harmonia Sacra*, Bk. II, 2nd ed., 1714. Organ parts   **1232, 1233**

God is gone up. *Boyce.* Organ parts   **1225, 1234**

*Hear my prayer. Organ parts   **1229, 1230**

*I cried unto the Lord. Organ part   **1233**

*I will alway give thanks. Organ part   **1232**

*I will sing. Organ part   **1235**

I waited patiently. Organ part with Treble Solo   **622**

     Organ part   **1234**

*Lord what love have I. Score   **23**

     Treble voice only   **683**

     Organ part   **1235**

*O be joyful. Organ part   **1233**

CROFT (William)—*continued*.

*O Lord God of my salvation. 4–6 voices. A. and T. only **1220–4**
        Organ part **1233**
*O Lord grant the King. Organ parts **1229, 1230**
*O Lord I will praise thee. Organ part **1232**
*O Lord rebuke me not. Organ part **1232**
*O Lord thou hast searched me out. Organ part **1232**
*Praise the Lord. Organ part **1234**
*Sing praises. Organ part **1233**
*Sing unto God. Organ parts **1232, 1235**
*Sing unto the Lord. T. and B. Chorus parts only **1220–4**
        Organ part **1234**
*The earth is the Lord's. Organ parts **1234, 1235**
*The Lord is my strength. Organ part **1234**
*Thou O God. A. T. B. Chorus parts only **1220–4**
        Organ part **1229**
*We wait for thy loving kindness. Organ part **1235**
*We will rejoice. Organ part **1230**
Part of the Music for the Oxford Act, July 13, 1713 (printed in *Musicus Apparatus Academicus*). Bass and Alto verse of 'With noise of Cannon,' and Alto verse of 'Laurus cruentas'; 1 and 2 Violins and Bass. Sep. **68–73**
When gentle sleep. 'The Dream.' Cantata for Bass Solo **1149**
Overture in G mi. for instruments, in 8 movements. 4 parts in score **620**
Overture in B♭ in 11 movements **620**
(In the first of these Overtures, the name is given as 'Craft'.)

CROSS (   ). Probably William Cross, born at Oxford in 1777. Succeeded Dr. Crotch as Organist of the Cathedral and University Church. Died 1825.

O God the protector of all. Organ part **1225**
Kyrie in E. Organ part **1225**

CROTCH (William). 1775–1847. Mus. Doc. Organist of Ch. Ch., 1790; Professor of Music in Oxford University, 1797.

The Anthems marked with an asterisk are printed in Crotch's *Ten Anthems, Respectfully Dedicated . . . To the Reverend The Dean and Chapter of Christ Church*, &c., *c.* 1798.

*Be merciful. F. A. for 4 v. Autograph **1226**
*God is our hope. V. A. for 2–4 v. **1226**
*How dear are thy counsels. F. A. for 4 v. Autograph **1226**
 I will cry unto God. V. A. for 4 v. Autograph **1226**
*O Lord God of Hosts. 4 v. Autograph **1226**
*Sing we merrily. 4 v. Autograph **1226**
 Seventy-one Chants. Autograph **1226**
 Fifteen Chants, twenty-six Hymn Tunes, and one Commandment Responses. Autograph **1143**

D

D. (W.).   These compositions belong to the middle of the 17th
   century.
Eight Almaines, 1 Coranto, 2 Sarabands.   In 3 parts.   Sep.
                                                     379–81

DAMAN (William), here also spelt 'Demaunde'.   Born in Liége.
   Came to England between 1561 and 1565.   Died 1591.   One of
   Queen Elizabeth's musicians.
O heavenly God.   Anthem for 5 v., wanting Bass   **56–60**
Confitebor tibi.   Motet for 5 v., wanting Tenor book   **979–83**
Omnis caro.   Motet for 6 v., wanting Tenor book   **979–83**
Prædicabo laudes.   Motet for 6 v., wanting Tenor book   **979–83**
Instrumental piece in 6 parts, wanting Tenor book   **979–83**

DAVY (John), of Exeter.
Double Chant   **1226**

DEANE (William).   A composer of the (?) early 17th century.
Short Service for 4 v.   Te D., Bdtus., Ky., Creed, Mag., N. Dim.
   Organ part, with words   **6**
Lord in thy wrath.   Organ part, with words   **6**
Blessed are those.   Anthem for 5 v. (Verse and Chorus).   Organ
   part, with words   **6**

DERING (Richard).   Mus. Bac., Oxford, 1610 ; Organist at Brussels,
   1617; Organist to Queen Henrietta Maria, 1625.   Died 1630.
Ten Motets for 2 v.   Printed in Playford's *Cantica Sacra*, 1662.
   Voice parts sep.   **747–9**

Ardens est cor.	Gratias tibi Deus.
Beatus vir.	Justus cor suum.
Canite Jehovæ.	O bone Jesu.
Ego dormio.	O Domine Jesu.
Gaudent in cælis.	Veni electa.

The same (without Beatus vir and Canite Jehovæ) with Basso.
   Sep.   **878–80**
Three Motets for 2 v.   Printed in Playford's *Cantica Sacra*, 1662.
   Conceptio tua.
   Duo Seraphim, wanting Basso continuo.
   Sancta et immaculata.
                    Sep.   **878–80**
Motet for 2 v.   Printed as Dering's in Playford's *Cantica Sacra*, the
   Second Set, 1674.
                    O crux ave.   Sep.   **878–80**
Nine Motets for 3 v.   Printed in Playford's *Cantica Sacra*, 1662.
   Sep.   **747–9**

DERING (Richard)—*continued*.

Cantate Domino.	O quam suavis.
Gloria Patri.	Panis angelicus.
Isti sunt sancti.	Qualis est dilectus.
Justus germinabit.	Vulnerasti cor meum.
Lætamini cum Maria.	

The same, without Gloria Patri, imperfect. Sep.　　**878–80**
Gloria Patri from the same, is also sep.　　**1013–5**
Cantica Sacra ad melodiam madrigalium elaborata senis vocibus, 1618.
　　The Basso continuo part of the whole book　　**1023**

Jubilate Deo.	Factum est silentium.
Vulnerasti cor.	Panis angelicus.
Sancta et immaculata.	O vos omnes.
Congratulamini mihi.	Cantate Domino.
Surge amica mea.	Quem vidistis.
Hei mihi Domine.	Veni Jesu.
Quæ est ista.	Paratum cor meum.
Adiuro vos filiæ.	Jesu decus angelicum.
Virgo prudentissima.	O crux ave.
Ardens est cor meum.	[Te laudamus] Te invocamus.
Quam pulchra es.	

If sorrowe might so fully be expreste. 6 v. Sep. parts, wanting
　　Bass　　**56–60**
Sleepe quiet Lee.　3 v.　S. T. B.　Sep.　　**747–9**
The citty Cryes.　5 v., wanting Bass　　**56–60**
Pavan in 4 parts 'for 2 Trebles'.　Sep.　　**423–8**
Three Phantasies, one Almaine, one Pavan, in 5 parts. Sep.　**423–8**
　　Of the same, those numbered 17 and 20 are in organ score　**1004**

DESGRANGES (　　).
Domine quid multiplicati sunt.　Sopr. Solo.　　**350**
Usque quo Domine.　Sopr. Solo.　　**350**

DIESNER, or DISINEER (Gerhard), fl. 1661–73.
Ground for Harpsichord　　**1177**

DIOMEDE (　　). Here called 'Signior' Diomede. Eitner
takes him to be Caton D., a Venetian, who went to Poland;
fl. 1606.

Four instrumental pieces in 4 parts, and three in 5 parts, one of
　　which is also ascribed to Cipriano de Rore.
Also Tirsi morir ; with 2nd part, Freno Tirsi ; and 3rd part, Così
　　morire, in 5 parts. Words in 1 Treble book only. Sep.　**372–6**

DIX (J.).
Nine Chants (3 with name ; 6 initialled)　　**1226**

DOUGLAS, or DOWGLAS (Patrick). A 16th-century composer, here described as 'priste, scotte borne'.

In convertendo, with 2nd part, Converte Domine.   Motet for 5 v. Sep., wanting Tenor Book   **979–83**
Ubi est Abel.   Motet for 5 v.   Printed *Musical Antiquary*, Oct. 1910.   Sep., wanting Tenor Book   **979–83**

DOWDON (John), of the second half of the 17th century.

Eight instrumental sets and pieces, of which three seem to be complete.   Tr. and Bass   **90–1**
One other, complete, in the same MSS., initialled J. D., is probably his.
Twenty-five instrumental pieces.   Violin part only   **361**
Three instrumental pieces, and another initialled J. D.   Violin part only   **362**

DOWLAND (John). 1563–1626. Lutenist and composer. Published between 1597 and 1614.

Two Songs from the *Second Book of Songs or Ayres*, 1600   **439**
    Come ye heavy stars (*sic*).
    Flow my teares, 'Lachrimæ Pavan'.
Three Songs from the *First Book of Songes or Ayres*, 1597   **439**
    If my complaint.
    Now O now.
    Sleepe wayward thoughts.

DUANTE (Leonora).

Seven Symphonies in 5 parts: 1, 2, 3, 8, 10, and 12 tones.   Sep. parts in one volume   **429**

DUETO (Antonio).   Chapel master at Genoa; fl. 1583–94.

Why should this worlds contentments. a 4.   S. A. T. B.   Sep.   **750–3**

DU FAUT, or DUFAULT.   A lutenist in England in the second half of the 17th century.

Corant for Harpsichord   **1236**

DUMONT (Henri).   1610–84.   Chapel master to Louis XIV.

Six Motets from the *Motets* of 1681.

            Desidero te millies.   4 v.   S. S. A. B.   Score   **83**
            Doleo super te.   3 v.   A. T. B.   **83**
            Duo Seraphim.   2 v.   **83**
                Extract from the same   **1124**
            Jesu dulcedo cordium.   3 v.   A. T. B.   **83**
            Jesu Rex admirabilis.   3 v.   A. T. B.   **83**
            O nomen Jesu.   2 v.   **83**
                Fragment of the same   **1124**

DUPUIS (Thomas Sanders). 1733–96. Mus. Doc. ; Organist of the Chapel Royal.

Two Chants   **1226**

E. (W.) ? William Ellis, q.v. These initials are stamped on the cover of 1113.

Lesson for Virginal   **1113**

ECCLES (John). Master of the King's Musick, 1700. Died 1735.

Belinda's pretty pleasing form : from 'Women will have their Wills'. Engraved by Cross, *c.* 1700. Treble voice only   **389**

I burn, my brain consumes, from 'Don Quixote', Part II. Treble voice only   **580**

A soldier, a sailor. Treble voice only   **360**

ECCLES (   ), probably John, q.v.

Overture and eight pieces for strings. Tenor and Bass only   **351–2**

ELLIS (William). Mus. Bac., 1639. Organist of Eton, and afterwards of St. John's Coll., Oxford. A. Wood refers to the Music meetings in his house during the Commonwealth.

Holy, holy. Organ part   **437**

O Lord our governour. Anthem for 4 v. Organ part (twice)   **437**

Three Almaines, 1 Corrant, 1 Serrabrand, and a piece called 'Michaelmas Day'. Bass only   **1022**

Thirteen pieces for Harpsichord, viz. :   **1236**

Five Almaynes (one called ' Almond Mariæ '); 2 Sarabrands (one called Mouline's Sarabrand set by W. E.) ; 4 Corants ; ' The Royallist ' ; ' Bow Bells '.

(Other pieces in this MS. are probably by Ellis.)

ELWORTH (   ), probably Jeffrey Elworth or Aleworth, one of Charles II's Violins (1674), and afterwards Musician for the Sackbuts. Died 1687. (See *The King's Musick.*)

Two Airs for the Violin. Violin part only   **362**

ESTE or EAST (Michael). Mus. Bac. Master of the Choristers at Lichfield. Published between 1601 and 1638.

Singe wee merily. V. A. for 6 v., with 2nd part ' Take the Psalm ', and 3rd part ' Blow up the Trumpet '. Sep. parts wanting Bass   **56–60**

When Israel came out of Egypt. V. A. for 5 v., with 2nd part, ' What aileth '. Organ part   **6**

(Both of these Anthems were printed by the Musical Antiquarian Society, edited by Rimbault.)

Four Fantazies in 5 parts   **716–20**

ESTWICK (Sampson). *c.* 1657–1739. Of Ch. Ch., Oxford; Minor Canon, Sacrist and Succentor of St. Paul's; Rector of St. Helen's, Bishopsgate, and St. Michael's, Queenhithe.

Julio festas referente luces. Song for the Oxford Act, 1–4 v., with instrumental parts in Score (see *Goodson, Richard*)   **619**

O Maria, O diva. Ode to Queen Mary. 1–4 v., with Overture and instrumental parts in Score   **619**

EVANS or EVINS (   )

Instrumental piece in 4 parts, Vo. 1 and 2, Vo., Bass   **1183**

FACCHO (Agostino). Organist at Bologna, 1624, and afterwards at Vicenza.

Three Motets from the *Motetti*, 1635   **623–6**
    Audite celi. 3 v. S. S. B.
    Exurgat Deus. 3 v. S. S. B.
    O sacrum convivium. 3 v. S. A. B.

Ave saluberrima. 4 v. from the same. Bass only   **880**

Questa ch' Orsola. 3 v. from *Madrigali*, 1636. Sep.   **623–6**

FARINA (Antonio); of the 2nd half of the 17th century.

Di due ciglia. Aria for Sopr. Solo   **956, 958**

FARINELLI (Cristiano). Violin player and composer, fl. 1680–1714.

Farinelli's Ground. 1st Violin only   **1183**

FARMELOE (Francis).

Instrumental piece, Bass only, incomplete   **21**

FARMER (John). Organist and Master of the Children of Christ Church, Dublin. Published between 1591–1601.

Looke up sad soule. 4 v. Sep.   **750–3**
(An adaptation of 'O stay swete loue' from his *First Set of English Madrigals*, 1599.)

FARMER (Thomas). One of the King's Musicians for the Violins, 1671; Musician in Ordinary, 1675. Mus. Bac., Cambridge, 1684. Died 1688.

Two Airs for the Violin. Violin part only   **361**

Four Airs for the Violin. Violin part only   **362**

Air (or perhaps Set of 3 Airs) in A ma. 1 Violin part only   **1183**

FARRANT (Daniel). One of the King's Musicians for the Violins, 1607–31; for the Lutes and Voices till 1641. Son of Richard Farrant, q.v.

Pauan upon fower notes. a 5   **423–8**
[Another Pavan 'Sacred Ende' in the same MSS. has the name 'Daniell' at end of Bassus, and 'T. Morley' in Cantus Book. The latter is probably meant.]

FARRANT (John). Organist of Ely, 1566; Hereford, 1592; Salisbury, 1598–1602.

    Kyrie and Creed. 'Mr. Farrant of Salisbury.' Organ part   88
    Te Deum. Organ part   88
          (Printed by Ouseley as by Richard Farrant.)

FARRANT (? John or Richard).

    Benedicity, apparently in Mode XIII and not part of John Farrant's service, nor of Richard Farrant's. Organ part   88

FARRANT (Richard). Master of the Children of St. George's, Windsor; Gent. of the Chapel Royal. Died 1580.

    Service in Mode IX. *Boyce.* Te D., Bctus., Ky., Creed, Mag., N. Dim. Score   1002
          Sep. parts, A. T. B. only   1220–4
          Bass part only   1012
          Organ part   1231
          The same without Ky. and Creed; short score   525
          Mag. and N. Dim. only. Organ part   88
    Call to remembrance. Anthem. 4 v. *Barnard, Boyce,* &c. Sep. A. T. B. only   1220–4
          Tenor only   440
          Organ parts   437, 438, 1001
          (For Aldrich's adaptation, see *Aldrich.*)
    Hide not thou thy face. Anthem. 4 v. *Barnard, Boyce,* &c. Sep. A. T. B. only   1220–4
          Score without words   1002
          Organ parts   1001, 437 (twice), 438
          (For Aldrich's adaptation, see *Aldrich.*)
    Lord for thy tender mercy's sake. Anthem. 4 v. *Cathedral Magazine,* &c. Sep. parts, A. T. B. only   1220–4
          Organ parts   437, 1225, 1230, 1235
          (See *Aldrich.* 'Not unto us.')
    When as we sate in Babilon. V. A. Organ part   6
    Ah, ah, alas! you salt sea gods. Pt. I. } 5 parts, for treble voice
    You Godds that guide. Part II. } and instruments.
          From a play dealing with Abradad and Panthea. Sep. parts   984–8

    [? By the waters of Babylon. See *Aldrich.*]

FAYRFAX (Robert). Mus. Doc.; Master of the Children of St. Albans Abbey; Gent. of the Chapel Royal. Died 1521.

    Ave Dei patris. Motet for 5 v. Sep. parts wanting Tenor book   979–83

FEDERICI (Francesco) of Rome: a priest who lived in the 2nd half of the 17th century.

    D'un bel ciglio. Cantata for Sopr. Solo   952
    Non sò se mi capite. Cantata for Sopr. Solo   952
    Son troppo stretti. Cantata for Sopr. Solo   952

FERRABOSCO (Alfonso) I.   Son of Domenico Maria Ferabosco.
   Born at Bologna, 1543. Settled in England before 1562. Returned
   to Italy in 1578, when he entered the service of the Duke of
   Savoy. Died at Bologna, 1588.

O remember not our oulde synnes. 6 v. By A. F., 'Senior.' Sep.
   parts, wanting Bass   **56–60**

Motets, &c.

De lamentacione.   5 v.   Sep., wanting Tenor book   **979–83**
         The same complete.   Sep.   **78–82, 463–7**
Mirabile mysterium.   5 v.   Sep. parts   **984–8, 78–82, 463–7**
Tribulationem et dolorem.   5 v.   Sep.   **984–8, 78–82**
      The following are anonymous here, but have been identified
   from other MSS.   There are probably other works by A. F. in
   these MSS.
Ad Dominum.   5 v.   Sep.   **78–82, 463–7**
Benedic anima mea.   Ps. civ.   Pt. I.   5 v.   Sep.   **78–82**
         Extendens cælum.   Pt. II.   4 v.   Sep.   **78–82**
         Qui fundasti.   Pt. III.   5 v.   Sep.   **78–82**
         Qui emittis.   Part IV.   5 v.   Sep.   **78–82**
         Rigans montes.   Part V.   4 v.   Sep.   **78–82**
         Saturabuntur ligna.   Part VI.   5 v.   Sep.   **78–82**
         Posuisti tenebras.   Pt. VII.   5 v.   Sep.
                                                   78–82, 463–7
         Quam magnificata.   Pt. VIII.   3 v.   Sep.   **78–82**
         Draco iste.   Pt. IX.   5 v.   Sep.   **78–82**
         Emittes spiritum.   Pt. X.   5 v.   Sep.   **78–82**
         Cantabo Domino.   Pt. XI.   Canon per diapason et
            diatesseron.   6 v.   Sep.   **78–82, 463–7**
Cantate Domino.   Pt. I.   5 v.   Sep.   **78–82**
         Quia beneplacitum.   Pt. II.   5 v.   Sep.   **78–82**
Conserva me.   Pt. I.   5 v.   Sep.   **78–82, 463–7**
         Vias tuas.   Pt. II.   5 v.   Sep.   **78–82, 463–7**
Da pacem.   6 v.   Sep. wanting Tenor book   **979–83**
Heu mihi Domine.   5 v.   Sep.   **78–82, 463–7**
Ingemuit Susanna.   5 v.   Sep.   **78–82, 463–7**
Judica me Domine.   Pt. I.   5 v.   Sep.   **78–82**
         Vide humilitatem.   Pt. II.   5 v.   Sep.   **78–82**
Miserere nostri.   5 v.   Sep.   **78–82**
Musica læta.   5 v.   Sep.   **78–82, 463–7**
Nuntium vobis.   5 v.   Sep.   **78–82**
Peccantem me.   5 v.   Sep.   **78–82, 463–7**
Surge propera.   Pt. I.   5 v.   Sep.   **78–82, 463–7**
         Surge propera.   Pt. II.   Sep.   **78–82, 463–7**

Madrigals.

Those marked with an asterisk * are in Ferrabosco's *Il primo libro
   de Madrigali,* 1587; those marked with a dagger † are in *Il
   secondo libro de Madrigali,* 1587.

FERRABOSCO (Alfonso) I—*continued*.
*Cara la vita.   5 v.   Sep.   78–82
*Chi ha cor.   5 v.   Sep.   78–82
†Donna l'ardente fiamma.   5 v.   Sep.   463–7
    (Also printed in *Musica Transalpina* II, 1597.)
        The same, 'Lady, my flame'.   Score without words   33
*Donna se voi.   5 v.   Sep.   78–82
    (Also printed in *Musica Transalpina* I, 1588.)
*Già fù mia.   5 v.   Sep.   78–82
    (Also printed in *Musica Transalpina* I, 1588.)
*Godea Tirsi.   5 v.   Sep.   78–82
    (Also printed in *Musica Transalpina* I, 1588.)
*Mentre ti fui si grato.   Pt. I.   5 v.   Sep.   78–82
    *Mentre ti fui si cara.   Pt. II.   5 v.   Sep.   78–82
    *Hor pien d'alto.   Pt. III.   5 v.   Sep.   78–82, 463–7
    *Hor un laccio.   Pt. IV.   5 v.   Sep.   78–82, 463–7
    (Also printed in Morley's Collection, 1598.)
    *Lasso donque.   Pt. V.   5 v.   Sep.   78–82
    *Ben che senza.   Pt. VI.   5 v.   Sep.   78–82
*Non fingo.   5 v.   Sep.   78–82
*O crude pene.   5 v.   Sep.   78–82
*O dolcissimo baccio.   5 v.   Sep.   78–82
    (Also printed in *Musica Transalpina* I, 1588.)
*Perle rubini.   5 v.   Sep.   78–82
    (Also printed in *Musica Transalpina* I, 1588.)
*Quanto io son.   5 v.   Sep.   78–82
*Se pur è ver.   5 v.   Sep.   78–82, 463–7
†Signor la vostra.   5 v.   Sep.   463–7
    (Also printed in *Musica Transalpina* II, 1597.)
    The same 'Sweet lord'.   Score without words   33
Tu dolce anima.   5 v.   Sep.   78–82
    (Printed in Pevernage's *Harmonia Celeste*, Antwerp, 1583.)
Vidi pianger.   Pt. I.   5 v.   Sep.   78–82
    Come dal ciel.   Pt. II.   5 v.   Sep.   78–82
    (Both printed in *Musica Transalpina* I, 1588.)
*Voi volete.   5 v.   Sep.   78–82
*Vorrei lagnarmi.   Pt. I.   5 v.   Sep.   78–82, 463–7
    *S'io taccio.   Pt. II.   5 v.   Sep.   78–82, 463–7
    (Both printed also in Morley's Collection, 1598.)
In nomine.   5 v.   Sep. (No. 24)   463–7
    (Cf. B. M. Add. MSS. 32377 and 29427.)

FERRABOSCO (Alfonso) II.   Son of Alfonso I.   One of the King's
    Musicians.   He composed music for some of Ben Jonson's
    Masques.   Buried at Greenwich, March, 1628.
Fuerunt mihi lacrimæ.   4 v.   Sep.   463–7
    The same, Tenor only   880
    (This is probably by A. F. II, not I).

FERRABOSCO (Alfonso) II—*continued.*

Laboravi in gemitu.   5 v.   Sep.   **463–7**
Rorate cæli.   3 v.   S. S. B.   Sep.   **623–6**
Heare me O God a broken hart, in 5 parts.   'Pavan' for Treble
 voice and instruments   **423–8**
     The same without words, called '4 notes pavan'
          527–30 and 1024

Sixteen songs from his *Ayres*, 1609.   Treble voice and Bass only
             439

Come away, come away.	O eyes O mortall starres.
Drowne not my teares.	Shall I seeke to ease my greife.
Fain I would.	Singe the nobles of his race.
Fly from the world.	Unconstante loue.
I am a lover.	Why stayes the bridegroom.
Iff all the ages of the earth.	With what new thoughts.
If all these cupides now.	Younge and simple though I am.
It was no pollicie of court.	Yes weare the loues.

Instrumental piece in 3 parts.
 Almaine   **379–81**

Instrumental pieces in 4 parts.
 Twenty fancies.   Sep.   **468–72**
    The same.   Sep.   **397–400, 517–20**
    The same.   Score   **2**
    Short Score   **436**
    Of these Nos. 1, 2, 11, 14, 15, 17, 18, 19, 20 are sep.
           423–8
    Nos. 6, 7, 8, 9, 10, 17, 18, 19 (Organ part) are in
           1004
    Part of Bass (unfinished) of No. 7   **67**
 Two Fancies (Pt. I 'Ut re mi'; and Pt. II) Pt. I printed in *Musical
 Antiquary*, January 1912.   Sep.   **397–400, 473–8, 517–20**
    Score   **2**
    Short Score   **436**
 Fantazia.   Organ Score   **1004**
    Sep. parts   **397–400**
    Score   **2**
    Short Score   **436**

Instrumental pieces in 5 parts.
 In nomine.   Sep.
   404–8, 423–8, 468–72, 527–30 and 1024, 716–20
    Organ   **1004**
    Short score   **436**
 In nomine.   Sep.
   404–8, 423–8, 468–72, 527–30 and 1024, 716–20
    Organ   **1004**
    Short score   **436**

FERRABOSCO (Alfonso) II—*continued.*
   In nomine ' 2 bases '.
        Sep.   **404–8, 468–72, 473–8, 527–30** and **1024**
        Short score   **436**
   In nomine (No. 14). Sep.   **423–8**
   ' Douehouse Pauan.' Sep.   **404–8, 423–8, 527–30** and **1024**
        Short Score   **436**
   ' 4 notes Pauan.' (See ' *Heare me O God* ' above.)
        Sep.   **404–8, 423–8, 527–30** and **1024**
        Score   **2**
        Short Score   **436**
   Two Pavans (Nos. 32 and 35). Sep.   **423–8**
        No. 35. Sep. **404–8,** Score **2,** Short Score **436**
   Almaine (No. 25). Sep.   **423–8**
        Treble and Bass only   **1114**
        Bass only   **1022**
   Almaine (No. 36).   **423–8**
        Sep.   **404–8**
        Score   **2**
        Short Score   **436**

   (Four more Pavans and an Almaine, Nos. 26, 27, 29, 31, 33, in **423–8**, perhaps by A. F. Of these No. 27 is in **404–8, 436** and **2.**)
   Two Fancies (Pt. I 'Ut, re, mi '; and Pt. II : 5-part versions of the same 4-part fancies). Sep.   **404–8**
        Score   **2**

Instrumental pieces in 6 parts
   Phantazia. Sep.   **404–8, 423–8, 473–8**
        Organ   **1004**
        Short Score   **. 436**
        Score   **2**
   Phantazia. Sep.   **61–66, 404–8, 423–8** (twice), **473–8**
        Organ   **1004**
        Short Score   **436**
        Score   **2**
   Fancy. Sep.   **61–6, 404–8**
        Score   **2**
        Short Score   **436**
   In nomine. Sep.   **61–6, 404–8, 473–8**
        Score   **2**
        Short Score   **436**

FERRABOSCO (John). Mus. Bac. Organist of Ely 1662. Died 1682.
   Almond, Corant and Sarabrand for Harpsichord   **1236**

FERRABOSCO (   ). It is not stated to which the following should be assigned. It is probably adapted from a Madrigal.
   Say God should send. 4 v. Sep.   **1074–7, 750–3**

FERRARA (Michael de).

Allman, cuntre dance (with probably Corant and Saraband). Violin
part only   **1066**

FILIPPI (Gaspare).   Chapel Master at Vicenza, 1637–53.

Three Motets from *Concerti Ecclesiastici*, 1637   **623–6**
     Intuens in cælum.   3 v.   A. T. B.
     O sacrum convivium.   3 v.   A. T. B.
     Vidi turbam magnam.   3 v.   B. B. B.

FINGER (Gottfried).   A native of Olmütz in Moravia.   Lived in
England *c.* 1685–*c.* 1701.

Instrumental piece (? Sonata).   Tenor and (unfinished) Bass only
                      351–2

FIOCCO (Antonio, *or* Pietro Antonio).   Born at Venice ; died at
Brussels, 1714.   Vice-master of the Court Chapel at Brussels,
1696.

Cæli dapes.   Motet for 1–4 v.   Score   **48**

FLORIO (Giovanni).   A composer of the 16th century.   Madrigals
by him appear in collections from 1566 onwards.

A pilgrym passinge.   3 v.   S.S.A.   **750–3**
O what have I deserved.   3 v.   S.S.A.   **750–3**

FONTANELLI (   ).   Probably Conte Alfonso, in the service
of Alfonso II d'Este ; fl. 1586–1608.

Padre del ciel.   5 v.   **510–4**

FONTEI (Nicolò).   Chapel master at Verona ; fl. 1635–47.

Et ecce sonuit, from *Melodiæ Sacræ*, 1638.   3 v.   A. T. B.
and Basso   **623–6**

FORCER (Francis).   *c.* 1650–*c.* 1705.   Contributed to Playford's
Choyce Ayres and Dialogues, 1679, &c.

Overture and eight tunes for strings.   Tenor and Bass only   **351–2**

FORCIL (   ).   Possibly a mistake for Forcer.

One tune for violin.   Violin part only   **362**

FORDE (Thomas).   Musician to Henry, Prince of Wales, and later
to Charles I.   Published *Musicke of Sundrie Kindes*, 1607.
Died 1648.

ANTHEMS AND SACRED MUSIC.

Those marked with an asterisk * seem to be imperfect, wanting
instrumental parts.
At night lye downe.   3 v.   **736–8**

FORDE (Thomas)—*continued*.

Bowe downe thine eare. 3 v.	**736–8**
Forsake me not. 3 v.	**736–8**
Glory be to the Father. 3 v.	**736–8**
Goe wounded soule. 3 v.	**736–8**
*Hayle holy woman (verse and chorus, 3 v.)	**736–8**
Heare my praier. 3 v.	**736–8**
How sitts this citty. 3 v.	**736–8**
Let us with lowde. V.A. 6 v., wanting Bass	**56–60**
Miserere my maker. F. A. 6 v., wanting Bass	**56–60**
My greifs are full. 3 v.	**736–8**
My sinnes are like. 3 v.	**736–8**
O clap your hands (Pt. I), with 2nd part, He shall chuse. 3 v.	**736–8**
O praise the Lord. 3 v.	**736–8**
Praise the Lorde, oh my soule. 3 v.	**736–8**
*Say bould but blessed theefe. 3 v.	**736–8**
*Strike Lord why wilt thow. Verse and Chorus. 3 v.	**736–8**
Strike thou the anvill. 3 v.	**736–8**
Why art thou so heavy. 3 v.	**736–8**
*Yet if his maiestie. 3 v.	**736–8**

MADRIGALS, &c.

*Are women fayre ? 3 v.	**736–8**
Come forth my deare. 3 v.	**736–8**
*Come let us enjoye. 3 v.	**736–8**
*Fire, fire, loe heare I burne. 3 v.	**736–8**
Greife, greife, keep in. 3 v.	**736–8**
Let not my blacknes. 3 v.	**736–8**
Musique devine. 6 v., wanting Bass	**56–60**
My love is like a garden. 3 v.	**736–8**
Now sleeps my love. 3 v.	**736–8**
Oh how my soule. 3 v.	**736–8**
Oh staye awhile. 6 v., wanting Bass	**56–60**
O thou whose loue. 3 v.	**736–8**
Our life is nothing. 3 v.	**736–8**
*Sigh no more ladies. 3 v.	**736–8**
Still shall my hopes. 6 v., wanting Bass	**56–60**
Sweet yet cruell. 3 v.	**736–8**
Tis now dead night. A passion on the death of Prince Henry. 6 v., wanting Bass	**56–60**
What curious face. 3 v.	**736–8**
What's a woman but her will. 3 v.	**736–8**
What greater joye. 3 v.	**736–8**
Whoever smelt the breath. 3 v.	**736–8**
Almayne for instruments. 3 parts sep.	**379–81**

FREE (   ), Dr.
Single Chant in B♭   **1229**

FREER (R. Lane).
Sanctus and Kyrie in G.   Organ part   **1225**

FRESCOBALDI (Girolamo).   1583–1644.   Organist of St. Peter's, Rome.
'Partite sopra Folia ad simbolum' for Virginal   **1113**

FULLER (   ).
Single Chant in B♮   **1226, 1229**

FUSETTI (Reverendo Padre).
Cum invocarem.   Motet for 1–4 v., with Accompaniment for 2 Violins.   Score   **385**
Dixit Dominus.   Motet for 1–4 v., with instrumental parts and Symphonies.   Score   **684**
Exurgite mortales.   Motet for Soprano, with 5 instrumental parts. Score   **388**
    (This is anonymous, but it evidently is part of the series 385–6–7.)
In te Domine.   Motet for 1–4 v., with Accompaniment for 2 Violins. Score   **386**
Magnificat anima for 1–4 v., with Accompaniment for 2 Violins. Score   **387**

GABRIELI (Giovanni).   1557–? 1612.   Organist of St. Mark's, Venice.
How long shall fadinge pleasure.   4 v.   **1074–7, 750–3**
My soule is deeply wounded.   3 v.   (Two copies of 1 and 2 Treble parts)   **739–43**

GAGLIANO (Marco da).   1602–42.   Chapel master of S. Lorenzo, Florence.   Composer of the opera *Dafne*.
Four Madrigals a 5, from the *First Book of Madrigals*, 1602   **510–4**
    Filli, mentre ti bacio.
    L'ardente tua facella.
    O sonno (Pt. I).
    Questo [sic. ; should be Ov' è il] silentio.

Madrigal from the *Fifth Book of Madrigals*, 1608.   Su la sponda. 5 v.   **510–4**

GALLERANO (R. P. Leandro).   Chapel Master of S. Antony, Padua; fl. 1620–8.

In Domino confido.   4 v.   Printed in J. Bapt. Aloysius's *Coelestis Parnassus*, 1628.   Basso continuo only **880**

GALLIARD (John Ernest).   *c.* 1687–1749.   A native of Zell, in Hanover.   Came to England about 1706.

The hymn of Adam and Eve (*Par. Lost*, Bk. V), for Sopr. and Tenor with Basso.   Printed 1728.   Score **77**
   V'cello part **73**
Cupid god of pleasing anguish.   Fragment of Treble voice only **960**
Ghosts of ev'ry occupation **960**
 (Songs from *Doctor Faustus or The Necromancer*, Printed 1724.)

GASPARINI (Francesco).   1668–1727.   Chapel Master of S. John Lateran, Rome.

E che farai.   Cantata for Sopr. Solo **993**

GERARDE (Derick).   A 16th-century writer, many of whose works exist in MS. in the British Museum Library.

Sive vigilem.   Motet for 6 voices.   Sep. parts, wanting Tenor book **979–83**

GIBBONS (Christopher).   1615–76.   Mus. Doc.   Son of Orlando, q.v.   Organist of Winchester Cathedral, 1638–44; of the Chapel Royal, and of Westminster Abbey, 1660.

Above the stars.   V. A.   Score **14**
 [The organ part of a different 'Above the Stars', ascribed to 'Christo. Gibbons', perhaps by error **92**]
Ah my soule.   3 v.   S. S. B.   Score **14**
   Score and sep. Treble parts **693**
God be mercyfull.   V. and Chos.   Scores **12, 14**
How long wilt thou forget.   V. A.   Printed in Playford's *Cantica Sacra*, II, 1674.   Score **12, 18**
   Sep. Chorus parts.   A. T. B. **1220–4**
   Sep. 1 and 2 Treble verses and Chorus.   A. T. B. **623–6**
O praise the Lord.   V. A.   Score **12, 14**
Sing unto the Lord.   V. A.   Printed in Playford's *Cantica Sacra*, II, 1674.   Score **12, 14**
Teach me O Lord.   V. A.   Printed in Playford's *Cantica Sacra*, II, 1674.   Score **14, 22**
The Lord said unto my Lord.   V. A.   Score **14, 22**
Celebrate Dominum.   2 v.   S. B.   Printed in *Cantica Sacra*, 1674. Score **18**

GIBBONS (Christopher)—*continued*.

Gloria Patri. 3 v. Score	**43, 48**
Laudate Dominum. Motet 4–6 v. Score	**14, 621**
O bone Jesu. Motet 4 v. Score	**14, 621**

Instrumental Music.

Four sets of 3 pieces (Fantasia, Allmaine, and Galliard), for 1 Treble and 1 Bass. Sep.	**414–16**
Organ part	**778**
Organ part, incompletely written out	**1180**
Score with organ	**8**
Bass only	**434**
Almaine, Corant, and Saraband for 1 Treble and Bass. Sep.	**414–6**
Score	**8**
Six sets of 3 pieces (Fantasia, Allmaine, and Galliard), for 2 Trebles and Bass. Sep.	**414–6**
Organ part, incompletely written out	**1180**
Score	**8, 620**
Seven ' Ayres ' or short pieces for 2 Trebles and Bass. Sep.	**414–6**
Score	**8**
The same. Nos. 1, 2, 3, 5, 6, Sep.	**1006–9**
Three Fantazias for 2 Trebles and Bass. Score	**21**
Four pieces in G mi. (not in **414–6**) ; Six in D mi. ; Four in D ma. for 2 Trebles and Bass	**1006–9**
Fancy a 4 (Vo. 1 and 2, Va. and Bass). Score	**8**
Alman and two other pieces (Nos. 7, 8, 9). Bass only	**434**
Two Voluntaries for Organ	**15, 47, 1176**
(Other pieces in these MSS. may be by him.)	
Piece for Organ or Harpsichord	**1003**
Piece for Organ or Harpsichord	**1179**

GIBBONS (Edward). Born *c*. 1570. Mus. Bac. Brother of Orlando Gibbons, q. v. Organist of King's Coll., Cambridge ; Bristol Cathedral ; and Exeter Cathedral.

Awake and arise. 3 v. Score	**43, 48**
Commandments and Creed to William Mundye's Short Service. Sep. A.; T. and B. Dec. and Cant.	**1220–4**

GIBBONS (Ellis). Brother of Orlando, q. v. Organist of Salisbury.

Long live faire Oriana. Madrigal for 5 v. from the *Triumphs of Oriana*, 1601. Score without words	**33**

GIBBONS (Orlando). 1583–1625. Organist of the Chapel Royal and of Westminster Abbey. The MS. **21** is for the most part in his autograph.

GIBBONS (Orlando)—*continued.*

SERVICES.

Short service 'for the organs, or without for a meane'. *Barnard, Boyce,* &c.   4 v.   Te D., Bdtus., Ky., Creed, Mag., N. Dim.

Score	**1002**
Short score	**525**
Organ part (with words)	**6**
Organ parts	**1001, 1231**
Sep. parts; A. T. B. only	**1220–4**
Te D., Bdtus., with Sanctus. Organ part	**1225**
Mag. and N. Dim.	**88**

Evening Service 'for verses'. *Barnard, Ouseley.*   Score   **1002**

Short score	**526**
Organ part	**1001**
Sep. parts; A. T. B. (Verse and Chos.) and T. (Chos.)	**1220–4**

First Preces and First Psalm, 'I will magnifie.'   A., A., T. B. sep.   **1220–4**

Second Preces and Second Psalm, 'The eies of all.'   (*Barnard's* 'First Preces'.)   A. T. B. sep. parts   **1220–4**
(The Preces 1 and 2 printed in *Ouseley.*)

ANTHEMS.

Almighty and everlasting God, mercifully looke.   ' 3rd Sunday after Epiphanie.'   *Barnard, Boyce.*   Organ part   **47**

Bass part only	**1012**

Almightie God which hast given.   'For Christmas Day.'   V. A.

Organ part	**1001**

Behold I bring you.   V. A.   *Ouseley.*

Sep. A. T. B., Verse and Chos., T. B. Chos. only	**1220–4**

Behold thou hast made.   ' This Anthem was made at the Intretie of Docter Maxcie Deane of Winsor the same day sennight before his death.'   V. A.   *Barnard, Ouseley.*   Printed by *Aldrich* as part of an intended publication.   Score   **12, 16, 21, 49**

Single Treble Voice part with Organ	**46**
Fragments of voice part (Treble)	**1114**
Alto solo part (ornamented) with Chorus parts compressed	**18**
Sep. Chorus parts, A. T. B. only	**1220–4**

Blessed are all they.   'A Weddinge Anthem first made for my Lord of Summersett.'   V. A.   *Ouseley.*   Score   **21**

Sep. A. T. B. Verse and Chos.; T. B. Chos.	**1220–4**
Organ part	**1001**

Deliver us o Lord, Pt. I
Blessed be the Lord, Pt. II } F. A.   4 v.   *Barnard, Ouseley.*

Bass voice part only	**1012**

E

GIBBONS (Orlando)—*continued.*

Glorious and powerful God. V. A. *Ouseley.* Score   **21**
        Sep. parts. A. and B., Verse and Chos.; Tr. and Tenor
          Chos.   **623–6**
        Sep. parts. B., Verse and Chos.; A. T. B., Chos. **1220–4**
        Organ part   **6**
Grant o holy Trinity. V. A. Organ part   **1001**
Great King of Gods. V. A. 'This anthem was made for the
    Kings being in Scotland.' *Ouseley*   **21**
Hosanna. 6 v. *Barnard: Boyce*, &c. Score   **16**
    Bass voice only   **1012**
    Short score without words   **525**
    Organ parts   **47, 1001, 1230, 1234**
If yee be risen. V. A. *Ouseley.*
    Organ parts **1001** (two copies, one unfinished); **1219**
Lift up your heads. 6 v. *Barnard:* organ part in *Ouseley.*
    Score   **16**
    Short score   **525**
    Bass only   **1012**
    Organ parts   **47, 1001, 1230**
Lord graunt grace. V. A. 'An Anthem for all saints day.' *Ouse-*
ley. Score   **21**
Lord wee besech thee 'for yᵉ Annuntiation of yᵉ Virgin Mary.'
    Organ part   **1001**
O God the King of glory. 'For Asention day.'
    Organ part   **1001**
O Lord in thee is all my trust. 'The Lamentation.' F. A. 5 v.
Ouseley. Score   **21**
Oh all true fathful harts. 'A thanks Giuing for the Kings happie
    recoverie from a great dangerous sicknes.' V. A. *Ouseley* as
    'O Thou the central orb'. Score   **21**
Out of the deepe. Organ part   **1001**
See the word is incarnate. V. A. 5 v. 'The words were made
    by Docter Goodman, De: of Rochester.' *Ouseley.* Score   **21**
        Sep. parts wanting Bass   **56–60**
Sing unto the Lord. 'Anthem of 5 Voc.: was made for Dᵒʳ Mar-
    shall.' *Ouseley.* Score   **12, 18, 21**
        Sep. parts. A., B. 1 and 2, Verse and Chorus; Tr. and
          Tenor Chorus   **623–6**
        Sep. parts. A., B. 1 and 2, Verse and Chorus; Tenor
          Chorus   **1220–4**
The Lord said. V. A. Sc.   **12**
This is the record of John. V. A. 'This Anthem was made for
    Dr. Laud, presedent of Sant Johns, Oxford.' *Ouseley.* Sc. **21**
Wee praise yee o father. V. A. *Ouseley.* Sc.   **21**
    Organ   **1219**
        Sep. A. T. B., verse and chos.; Bass chorus **1220–4**

GIBBONS (Orlando)—*continued.*

Hymns from George Wither's *Hymnes and Songs of the Chvrch,* 1623.

1. Now shall the praises.	10. O Lord of Hoastes.
2. Sing praises Israel.	11. How sad and solitary.
3. Now in the Lord.	12. Lord, thy answere.
4. Thy beauty Israel.	13. Thus Angels sung.
5. Come kisse me.	14. Oh all you Creatures.
6. Oh my Loue, how comely.	15. Come Holy-Ghost.
7. Arise thou North-winde.	16. A Song of Joy.
8. Who's this, that leaning.	17. When one among the Twelve.
9. Lord, I will sing.	

Two parts in Score	**365**
Bass part only	**366**

The whole contents of *The First Set of Madrigals*, 1612.   Score without words   **21**

The silver swan.	Mongst thousands good. Pt. II.
O that the learned Poets.	Now each flowry bancke.
I waigh not Fortune's frown, Pt. I.	Lais now old.
I tremble not, Pt. II.	What is our life?
I see ambition, Pt. III.	Ah deere hart.
I faine not friendship, Pt. IV.	Faire is the Rose.
How art thou thral'd.	Nay let me weepe. Pt. I.
Farewell all joyes.	Yet if that age. Pt. III.
Daintie fine Bird.	Nere let the Sunne. Pt. II.
Faire Ladies that to Love, Pt. I.	Trust not too much.

Instrumental Music.

Nine three-part Fancies from *Fantazies of III parts*, wanting 1st Treble. Sep.	**401–2**
Score	**2**
The same, excepting No. 3. Score	**21**
Sep. parts	**61, 64, 66**
The first six of the same. Sep.	**473–8**
Four of the same (Nos. 2, 3, 6, and 7), being respectively Nos. 1, 2, 5, and 6 in the engraved book	**459–62**
The 1st and part of the 8th of the engraved book. Organ part	**15**
The 8th of the same called 'Voluntarie' for Organ	**47, 1176**
Four three-part Fancies	**419–21**
The same, called his 'musique for the Great Dooble Basse'	**732–5**
Two four-part Fancies (for the Great Double Basse)	**732–5**
The same, wanting 2nd Treble book	**419–21**

GIBBONS (Orlando)—*continued.*

Two In nomines. a 5	**423–8**
The 1st of these also in	**404–8**
Score	**2**
Short score	**436**

Four six-part Fantasias (or Madrigals without the words?). The beginning of the 1st is missing. The name of Orlando Gibbons is on the 4th only. Score   **21**

ORGAN AND VIRGINAL MUSIC.

'Whoope doe me no harme good man'	**431**
Voluntarie of foure parts; Preludium; The Queenes Command; A Runing fantazia	**47**

    (Of these, 'Preludium' and 'The Queenes Command' were printed in *Parthenia*, 1611.) The 'Preludium' is also in **89**

    The 'Voluntarie of foure parts' is also in   **1176**

Eight pieces for Virginal, 5 unnamed (Nos. 63, 65, 66, 68, and 72); An Aire (No. 89); Galliard (99); Allmaine (97)   **1113**

    Of these, the 'Aire', 89, is in   **1003**

The Sarabrand (*sic*) of Orlando Gibbons	**1175**
Fantazia, a 4, for Organ	**1141–2**
Welcom home	**437**

'The crye', Pt. I, and 'A good sawsedg', Pt. II (probably madrigals) for keyboard instrument   **67**

GIBBONS (   ) ? Christopher or Orlando.

Sing we merrily. Organ part   **1230**

GIBBS (R.), probably Richard. Organist of Norwich Cathedral, ? 1622–30.

Allmaine and Corant for Virginal   **1177**

GILES (Nathaniel). Mus. Doc. Chorister at Magdalen Coll., Oxford, 1559–61; Clerk there, 1577; Master of the Children of St. George's, Windsor, and of the Chapel Royal. Died 1633.

SERVICES.

Te D., Jub., Ky., Creed, Mag., and N. Dim. 'for verses'. *Barnard.* Sep. A. (Dec.) T. and B. (Dec. and Cant.)   **1220–4**

Mag. and N. Dim. of the same. Organ part   **1227**

Mag. and N. Dim., 'his new service for verses'. Sep. A. (Dec.) T. and B. (Dec. and Cant.)   **1220–4**

ANTHEMS, &c.

O give thanks. F. A. *Barnard.* A. T. B. only. Sep.   **1220–4**

    Organ part   **1001**

GOODALE (Stephen).   Probably Chaplain at Ch. Ch.   Died 1637.
  See Foster's *Alumni*.

Ayre for instruments.   Bass part only   **1022**

GOODENOUGH (R. P.).   Twenty-five Chants   **1226**

GOODSON (Richard), senior.   1655–1718.   Mus. B.   Organist of
  Christ Church ; Professor of Music in the University.   Most of
  the following appear to be his original MSS.

SERVICES AND ANTHEMS.

Morning Service in C.   Te D. and Jub.   Verse and Chos.   Score
  (with 3 versions of the *Gloria* to Jubilate)   **616**
                    Organ part   **1231**
Evening service in F.   Cantate and D. Mis.   V. and Chos.   Score
                                                               1173

Single chant.   4 v.   Score   **48**
Blessed is he.   V. Anthem.   Score   **22**
                    (Two copies, one inserted loose.)
I am well pleased.   V. Anthem.   Score   **1219**
Not unto us.   V. Anthem.   Score   **1219**
Rejoyce in the Lord.   V. Anthem.   Score, with sep. Chorus
  parts, S. A. T. B. ; and Instr. parts, Vo. 1 and 2, Va., and
  Bass   **1219**
  Songs for the Oxford Act for solo voices and Chorus, with
  Symphonies and Instrumental Accompaniments in score.
Carminum præses.   **621**
            Another copy differing somewhat,   **618**
            in which is inserted a 3rd copy (? in Aldrich's hand-
            writing) more nearly resembling that in **621**.   The
            name of 'Aldrich' is written in pencil on **618** and
            621 in a modern hand, but the lettering on the back
            of **618**, 'Act Songs composed by Rich^d. Goodson,
            sen^r.,' makes it evident that he is the composer.

Jam resurgit Divus.   **618**
O cura Divum.   **618**
O qui potenti.   **617**
Quis efficaci carmine.   **618**
Sacra musarum.   **618**
Janus did ever to thy wondring eyes.   'After the victory at Blenheim.'
  Score   **618**
            Fragments of the same   **616**
Ormond's glory, Malbrough's arms.   Score   **617**
Overture.   'This Overture was compos'd for an Act song, Set to
  music by Mr. Sampson Estwick,' probably ' Julio festas referente
  luces' (q.v.), which is in the same key, F.   Score   **618**
Various instrumental pieces in B♭, perhaps a suite.   Score   **618**

GRABU (Lewis). A French composer who seems to have come to England at the Restoration, being named as ' Master ' of the King's Musick in 1660, and 'Composer' in 1665. He died about 1687. See *The King's Musick*.

Air for the violin. Treble only **362**

GRANDI (Alessandro), fl. 1610–37. Maestro di Cappella in Santa Maria Maggiore at Bergamo.

O bone Jesu. 4 v. From *Il secondo libro de Motetti*, 1628. Also printed in Playford's *Cantica Sacra*, 1662. Sep. parts **747–9**
    Basso only **880**
Basso (organo) part of 4-part Motetts from Grandi's printed collections. **880**

> From *Il primo libro de Motetti*, 1628 :
> Benedictus Dominus.
> Cantate Domino.
> Caro mea.
> Congratulemini.
> Hic est vere Martyr.
> Obaudite me.
> Vidi spetiosam.

> From *Il secondo libro de Motetti*, 1628 :
> Heu mihi.
> Inter vestibulum.
> Magnum hæreditatis.
> O bone Jesu (see above).

> From *Il Quarto libro de Motetti*, 1628 ;
> Deus qui nos.
> Diligam te Domine.
> Plorabo.

> From *Il sesto libro de Motetti*, 1630 :
> Domine in furore.

(The dates given above are those of the editions of which copies are in this Library.)

GRATIANI (Bonifatio). 1605–64. Maestro di Cappella to the Chiesa del Gesù and Seminario Romano at Rome. (*Eitner*.)
The contents of MS. **7** are copied from the six books of *Motetti a voce sola*.

(6) Ad cantus. Tr. Solo **7**
(1) Ad cœlestem Jerusalem. Tr. Solo **7**
(4) Ad laudes. Tr. Solo **7, 17**
(5) Ad matrem. Tr. Solo **7**
(6) Advenisti. Tr. Solo **7**
(4) Allelujah, de funere. Tr. Solo **7, 17**
(2) Alma redemptoris. Tr. Solo **7**
(4) Anima mea. Tr. Solo **7, 350**

GRATIANI (Bonifatio)—*continued.*

(6) Applaudite. Tr. Solo   7
(3) Ardens est. Bass Solo 7
(1) Ardet amans. Tr. Solo 7
(6) Attendite verbum. Tr. So'o
    7
(5) Audi clementissime. Tr.
    Solo 7
(4) Canite filiæ. Tr. Solo
    7, 17
(6) Cœli cives. Tr. Solo   7
(3) Cœli duces. Tr. Solo   7
(4) Crudelis infernus. Tr.
    Solo 7, 17
(1) Dedit abissus. Bass Solo 7
    The same, with English
    words, 'They that go
    down,' adapted by Dr.
    Pickering 48
(2) Diem festum. Tr. Solo 7
(2) Dilecte mi. Tr. Solo   7
(3) Dominus illuminatio. Tr.
    Solo 7
(5) Dum sederet beatus. Tr.
    Solo 7
(2) Erumpe Mariam. Tr. Solo
    7
(2) Erumpite flammæ. Tr.
    Solo 7
(2) Exulta jubila. Tr. Solo 7
(3) Florete prata. Tr. Solo 7
(6) Flos Romanarum. Tr.
    Solo 7
(1) Fremite, currite. Tr. Solo 7
(6) Gaude cor. Tr. Solo   7
(2) Gaude exulta. Tr. Solo 7
(1) Gaudia pastores. Tr. Solo
    7
(2) Germinate campi. Tr. Solo
    7
(2) Hæc est læta. Tr. Solo 7
(1) Hodie collætantur. Tr.
    Solo 7
(4) Ibat in accessos. Tr. Solo
    7
(3) Jacebam. Tr. Solo   7

(1) Laboravi. Tr. Solo   7
(5) Magnificate. Tr. Solo 7
(5) Multiplicatæ. Tr. Solo 7
(1) O cor meum. Tr. Solo 7
(4) O dulcis Jesu. Tr. Solo
    7, 350
(5) O hilaris. Tr. Solo   7
(6) O quam pulcher. Tr. Solo
    7
(4) Per asperos. Tr. Solo
    7, 350
(1) Plaudite vocibus. Tr. Solo
    7
(3) Quam dilecta. Tr. Solo 7
(1) Quam pretiosa. Tr. Solo 7
(1) Quasi sol. Tr. Solo   7
(3) Quicumque amat. Tr. Solo
    7
(6) Quis me territat. Tr. Solo
    7
(3) Regina cœli. Tr. Solo 7
(2) Rorate nubes. Tr. Solo 7
(4) Salve cœlitum. Tr. Solo
    7, 17
(1) Salve regina (1). Tr. Solo 7
(6) Salve regina (2). Tr. Solo 7
(5) Sinite me. Tr. Solo   7
(5) Si quis diligit. Tr. Solo 7
(6) Sponsa sua. Tr. Solo 7
(4) Surge dilecte. Tr. Solo
    7, 17
(6) Surrexit pastor. Tr. Solo 7
(6) Tormentorum sævitiam.
    Tr. Solo 7
(4) Ubi est dilectus. Tr. Solo
    7
    Velut palma. Tr. Solo 17
(3) Venerat illa dies. Tr. Solo 7
(6) Veni gaude. Tr. Solo 7
(6) Venite audite. Tr. Solo 7
(4) Venite pastores. Tr. Solo
    7
(3) Vidi Luciferum. Tr. Solo 7
(2) Volate cœlites. Tr. Solo 7
(2) Vos qui statis. Tr. Solo 7

    ('Velut palma' and 'Venite pastores' are printed in Playford's
Harmonia Sacra, Bk. II, 1693.)

GRATIANI (Bonifatio)—*continued*.

Sub umbra noctis.   Bass Solo with 3 instr. parts.   Score   83

   The whole contents of *Motetti a due e tre voci*, 1667.   Score   83

Venite gentes. 2 v.	Surge veni. 3 v.
Surrexit Christus. 2 v.	Mille tormenta. 3 v.
Hic est panis. 2 v.	Adeste turba. 3 v.
Omnes gentes. 2 v.	Ave millies beata. 3 v.
Domine ne in furore. 3 v.	Transeamus pastores. 3 v.
Hæc est vera fraternitas. 3 v.	Convertemini ad me. 3 v.

GREENE (Maurice). 1695–1755. Mus. Doc. Organist of St. Paul's
   and the Chapel Royal.

   The following anthems are all in *Forty Select Anthems in Score*
   except 'Like as the hart'.

Acquaint thyself with God.   Score (unfinished)   **1111**

          Treble voice part   **1111**

          Organ parts   **1233, 1234, 1235**

Blessed are those.   Organ part   **1229**

Hear O Lord.   Organ part   **1233, 1235**

I will seek unto God.   Organ part   **1234**

I will sing of thy pow'r.   Organ parts   **1229, 1233**

Let my complaint.   Organ part   **1229**

Like as the hart.   *Arnold.*   Organ part   **1234**

Lord let me know mine end.   Organ part   **1232**

My God, my God look upon me.   Organ part   **1233**

My soul truly waiteth.   Organ part   **1235**

O God of my righteousness.   Organ part   **1234**

O God thou art my God.   Organ part   **1232**

O Lord give ear.   Organ part   **1229**

O praise our God ye people.   Organ part   **1232**

O sing unto the Lord.   Organ part   **1233**

Praise the Lord O my soul.   Score   **22**

          Organ part   **1234**

The King shall rejoice.   Organ part   **1235**

The Lord is my shepherd.   Organ part   **1234**

Single chant in B♭   **1226, 1229**

Single chant in G   **1226**

The Fly.   Song.   Treble voice part only   **1111**

GREVILLE (   ).

Double chant in A   **1226**

GUAMI (Gioseffo or Giuseppe) of Lucca. Organist to Duke Albrecht
   of Bavaria; to Gian Andrea Doria at Genoa; 2nd Organist of
   St. Mark's, Venice; Organist of the Duomo at Lucca. Died 1611.
   (*Eitner.*)

Pittie my woes.   Treble and Alto   **740–2**

HALL (Henry), *c.* 1655–1707. Organist of Exeter; and of Hereford.

Te Deum in E♭.   3–4 v. *Arnold,* &c. (See *Hine* ; *Hayes.*)
    Score   **42**
    Organ part   **1232**
Two Chants   **1229**
Praise the Lord O ye servants.   Organ part   **1233**
Fill the bowl with rosie wine.   3 v.   Score.   **350**
Hast Charon hast, 'tis Nol.   A Dialogue between Oliver and Charon.   Tr., Bass, and Basso   **49**
    Voice parts, incomplete   **389**
No sullen cloud.   Dialogue between a Shepherd and Shepherdess, Tr. and Bass with 3 instrumental parts.   Score   **1212**
To our arms on earth.   'A health.'   Tr. and Bass   **1219**
While he in tryumph.   'Song to ye Queen' (Anne).   Soli and Chorus, with Overture and Instr. parts.   Score   **1212**
Air for instruments, 2 Trebles and Bass.   'Mr.' Hall   **90–1**
    The 1st Tr. part of the same   **362**
Two tunes (Violin part only).   'Mr.' Hall   **361**

HAMPDEN (Mrs. Elizabeth).

I must complayne.   Song for Treble with Bass.   (2 copies, pp. 62 and 68)   **439**

HANDEL (George Frederick).

Te Deum and Jubilate (*Utrecht*).   Treble chos. parts   **68, 69**
    Te Deum only, Tenor chos. part, incomplete   **72**
As pants the hart.   Score   **615**
    Treble chos. part   **1082**
    Sep. parts.   (Tr. and Tenor chos.; Vo. 1 and 2; Cello; Violone Grosso (incomplete); Hautboy; Bassoon)   **69–75**
I will magnifie thee.   Sep. parts.   (Vo. 1 and 2, Cello, Bassi and Hautboy)   **70, 71, 73–5**
    Hautboy part transposed   **1141**
Let thy hand be strengthened.   Treble chos. part   **69**
O praise the Lord with one consent.   Treble chos. part   **69**
O sing unto the Lord.   Sep. parts.   (Vo. 1 and 2, Cello, Bassi and Hautboy)   **70, 71, 73–5**
The King shall rejoice.   Treble chos. part   **69**
The Lord is my light.   Treble chos. part   **69**
Zadok the priest.   Organ part   **1111**
Chant (from Handel)   **1226**
Acis and Galatea.   Choruses with Instr. Accompts.   Score   **622**
    O the pleasure.
    Wretched lovers.
    Mourn all ye Muses.
    Must I my Acis ; Cease Galatea.
    Galatea dry thy tears (without words).

HIGGINS (   ).
Double Chant in F   **1226**

HILL (Roger).   Gentleman of the Chapel Royal, 1661–73.
The thirsty earth. Song for Bass voice with two Treble parts added
by Edward Lowe, q. v.   The original song is in Playford's *Select
Airs and Dialogues*, Bk. II, 1669   **17**

HILTON (John).   Mus. Bac.   Organist of Trin. Coll., Cambridge.
Died *c.* 1612.
Faire Oriana, Madr. a 5.   From *The Triumphs of Oriana*, 1601.
Score without words   **33**

HILTON (John), 1599–1657.   Organist of St. Margaret's, West-
minster.   Published *Ayres or Fa La's*, 1627 ; and *Catch that
catch can*, 1652.
The earth is the Lord's.   Anthem 'for 4 Basses'.   Sep. parts. A.
B. B. B. B. only   **1220–4**
Preludium and 5 Fantazias in 3 parts.   Sep.   **744–6**
Boy go up.   3 v. (a catch)   **1114**

HINE (William).   1687–1730.   Organist of Gloucester Cathedral.
Jubilate in E♭ (to Hall's *Te Deum*, q. v.   See *Hayes*).   *Arnold.*
Score   **42**
Organ   **1232**
Chant   **1229**

HINGSTON (John).   Organist to Oliver Cromwell; one of Charles II's
musicians.   Died 1683.
Voluntarie for Organ   **47, 1176**

HINTON (James).   Unknown.   A 'John' Hinton was organist of
Newark ; d. 1688.
Pieces in 3 parts, for 2 Trebles, Bass and Basso.   Pavan, Almaine,
Corant, Sarabrand, Pavan, Ayre, Corant, Sarabrand.   Sep.
1006–9

HOLLAND (William W.), 1807.   'Hertford Coll.'
Seven Chants   **1226**

HOLMES (George).   Organist of Lincoln Cath. 1704.   Died 1721.
I will love thee O Lord.   V. A.   Score   **621**

HOLMES (John).   Organist of Winchester Cath., and of Salisbury,
1602–10.
Magnificat.   'Mr. Holmes in Gamut.'   Organ part   **88**
O Lord of whome I do depend.   V. A.   Organ part   **88**
Pavan for instruments in 3 parts.   Sep.   **379–81**
Fantazia for Virginal   **1113**

HOLMES (J.).
Seven Chants   **1226**

HOLMES (Thomas).
Sarabrand for Harpsichord   **92**
    A piece called 'Puddinge', initialled T. H. may also be his.

HOLT (   ).   ? A writer of the end of the 17th century.
Eight instrumental pieces in 4 parts.   3 in G mi.; 3 in A mi.; 2 in
    D mi.   Vo. 1 and 2, Va., Bass   **1183**

HOOPER (Edmund). Master of the Children of Westminster Abbey,
    1588; Gentleman of the Chapel Royal. Died **1621**.

Behold it is Christ.   5 v.   *Barnard*.   Score   **16**
    Short score without words   **525**
    Sep. A. T. B. only   **1220–4**
    Organ parts   **6, 47, 1230**
Harken ye nations. (For the 5th of November). V. A. for 6 v.
    Sep., wanting Bass   **56–60**
    Sep. A.; T. and B. Cant. and Dec. only   **1220–4**
I will magnifie thee.   5 v.   Bass voice only   **1012**
    Score   **48**
    Organ part   **1001**
O God of Gods. V. A.   Sep. A. T. B. only   **1220–4**
The blessed Lambe. V. A.   5 v.   Sep. wanting Bass   **56–60**
Teach me thy way. *Barnard*. Bass part only   **1012**

HUDSON (George). Musician to Charles I for Lutes and Voices;
    to Charles II for violins. He appears to have been dead in 1678;
    see *The King's Musick*.

Two sets of instrumental pieces, a 2. (Treble, Bass and Tho. Bass.).
    (i) Almaine, Corant, Sarabrand, Country Daunce.
    (ii) Almaine, Corant, Sarabrand, A Frisk.
Three sets of pieces, a 3.   (2 Trebles, Bass and Tho. Bass).
    (i) Galliard, Pavan Almaine, Almaine, Corant, Corant.
    (ii) Pavan Almaine, Almaine, Galliard, 2 Corants, 2 Sara-
        brands, Passigaglia, Sarabrand.
    (iii) Pavan, Almaine, Ayre, unnamed piece, Corant, 2 Sara-
        brands, Country Daunce   **1006–9**

HUMFREY (Pelham). One of the Children of the Chapel Royal
    under Captain Cooke, 1660; Gentleman of the Chapel Royal,
    1667; Master of the Children, 1672. Died **1674**.

Service in E mi.   Te D., Jub., Mag., N. Dim.   Organ part   **1231**
Single Chant [known as *Grand*]   **48 and 1226**
Haste thee O Lord. V. A.   Score   **12**
Have mercy upon me. V. A.   *Boyce*. Score   **621**
Hear my crying. V. A. with Instr. Symphonies.   Score   **628**
Like as the hart. V. A.   *Boyce*. Score   **12, 22**

HUMFREY (Pelham)—*continued*.

O be joyful. V. A. Score	12
O give thanks. V. A. for with Instr. Symphonies. Score	628
O praise the Lord, laud ye. V. A. with Instr. Symphonies Score	628
The king shall rejoice. V. A. with Instr. Symphs. Score	628
Thou art my king. *Boyce*. V. A. with Instr. Symphs. Score	628

Songs, &c.

Hark how the wakeful. ' A dialouge between 2 penitents.' ' Begun by Mr. Humphreis, and finished by Dr. John Blow.'   Printed in Playford's *Harmonia Sacra*   49

How well does this harmonious meeting. Treble Solo and Chos. Score   43, 350

Lord I have sinn'd. *Harmonia Sacra*, Bk. I   49, 350

O the sad day. Sopr. Solo. *Harmonia Sacra*   49, 350

Wilt thou forgive the sin. *Harmonia Sacra*   49, 350

A poor soul sat sighing. (A parody of Humfrey's song, printed in Playford's *Musical Companion*, 1686)   1154

HUSBANDS (Will.). Copyist of Bass songs ' Audite me ' by Sances, and ' Dulcis amor ' in   1151

O Lord rebuke me not. An adaptation to new words of Robert White's The Lord bless us. q. v. Score   11, 16
        Organ part   1230

Come Holy Ghost. T. and B. only   1220–4

INDIA (Sigismondo d'). Born at Palermo. Was in the service of the Duke of Savoy; fl. 1606–27.

In principio creavit, a 4, from *Liber Primus Motectorum*, 1627. Score   48

Twenty Madrigals from *Il Quinto Libro de Madrigali a cinque voci*, 1616. Sep. wanting Tenor book   721–4

Felice Primavera. Pt. I.	Quando mia cruda sorte.
Danzan le Ninfe. Pt. II.	La doue sono.
Fugg' io quel disleale	Madonna vdite.
Quel neo, quel vago neo.	Cura gelata.
Quando quel bianco lino.	Hoggi nacque.
Quando tra le dorate nubi. Pt. I.	Soura le verdi chiome.
Riso tu. Pt. II.	Io mi sento morir.
Ecco l'onde d'argento.	La giouinetta. Pt. I.
Sospir che del bel petto.	E l'ombra fresca. Pt. II.
Amor fatto di neve.	Le piu belle Citelle.

INGLOTT (William). 1554–1621. Organist of Norwich Cathedral.

Te Deum. Organ part   1001

ISAAK (Bat. or Bartholomew).   Child of the Chapel Royal under
    Blow, 1674–7.   See *The King's Musick*.   Composer of V. A.
    'I will love Thee' in B. M. Add. MS. 17840.

Double Chant (twice entered)   **437, 1229**
Single Chant   **48**
Single Chant   **437**

IVE or IVES (Simon).   1600–62.   Vicar Choral of St. Paul's : con-
    tributed Catches, Songs, &c., to the publications of the day.

Boy go down.   Catch for 3 v.   **1114**
Sad clouds of grief.   'An Elegie on yᵉ Death of the Renowned and
    worthy Gent., William Austin of Lincolnes Inne, Esquire.'   3 v.
    Tr. Tenor, Bass.   Sep.   **736–8**

INSTRUMENTAL MUSIC.

In 3 parts.   A Pauan : The Wagg; Coranto; Seraband.
          Sep.   **379–81**
Ten pieces for Liero Violls, one part only   **727**
        Mris Mary Browne's Choyce, Coranto, Mris Collier's Choyce,
    The Choyce, Mris. Anne Forest's Choyce, The man in yᵉ Moone,
    Sir Will. Owen's Choyce, All you forsaken louers, and two un-
    named.
In 4 parts.   Two Pavans   **367–70**
In 5 parts.   Two In Nomines   **716–20**
           The first of these is also in   **473–8**
           Fantazia   **423–8**
In 6 parts.   Fancy   **61–66**

JACKSON (John).   Organist and Vicar at Wells Cathedral, 1674–88.
    Two Anthems by him are printed in Playford's *Cantica Sacra*,
    1672.   See West, *Cathedral Organists*.

Gloria Patri.   a 4 with Basso Continuo   **1201**
Magna et miranda.   a 3 with Basso Continuo   **1201**

JACKSON (William), of Exeter.   Double Chant   **1226**

JEFFERIES or JEFFREYS (George).   According to Anthony Wood,
    steward to Lord Hatton of Kirbie, Northants, and organist to
    Charles I at Oxford.

Erit gloria Domini.   2 v.   S. and T.   Score   **18**
    (Printed in Playford's *Cantica Sacra*, 1674).
Six Phantasias for 2 Trebles and Bass.   Sep.   **468–72**
The first four of these also in   **459–62**
Sing wee merilie.   F. A.   5 v.   Cf. B.M. Add. MS. 30479 (Tenor
    only) where it is attributed to 'Mr. Jefferies'.   Bass only **1012**
[Heu me miseram.   Dialogue of Maria et Angelus.   S. B. Attributed
    to Jefferies in B.M. Catalogue (cf. Add. MS. 29282), but the
    ascription is doubtful   **18**]

JEFFREY or **JEFFREYS** (Matthew). Vicar Choral of Wells. Mus. Bac. Oxford, 1593–4.

If the Lord himself. V. A. a 6. Wanting Bass. Sep.	**56–60**
Lord remember David. Full A. a 6. Wanting Bass. Sep.	**56–60**
My love is crucified. Full A. a 5. Wanting Bass. Sep.	**56–60**
Out of the deep. V. A. a 6. Wanting Bass. Sep.	**56–60**
Praise the Lord. V. A. Sep. A. T. (Dec. and Cant.), B. (Dec. and Cant.) only	**1220–4**
Singe wee merrily. V. A. a 6. Wanting Bass. Sep.	**56–60**

JENKINS (John). 1592–1678. One of Charles II's Musicians. (See *The King's Musick*.)

Fair Aristilla. Dialogue of Cleon and Aristilla. Incomplete, without Basso	**736–8**
See the bright light. 2 v. Treble and Bass	**17**
Victorious tyme. Tr. and Bass with Basso	**623–6**
Bass voice only	**366**
Wellcome pure thoughts. Tr. and Bass with Basso	**623–6**
Bass voice only	**366**
Sacred pieces for 3 voices. Sep.	**736–8**

And art thou greeved. A. A. B.	O nomen Jesus. A. A. B.
Awake sad hart. A. A. B.	O sacred teares. Tr. A. B.
Bright spark, shot. Tr. A. B.	O take thy lute. A. A. B.
Cease my soule. A. A. B.	Tell me my love. A. T. B.
Glorie honor powre. A. A. B.	The shephards sing. A. A. B.
Holy and blessed Spirit. A. A. B.	Then with our trinity. Tr. A. B.
Mercie dear Lord. Tr. A. B.	Tune me O Lord. A. T. B.
No, no, he is not gone. A. A. B.	Vain-glorious peece. A. A. B.
O Domine Deus. A. A. B.	

INSTRUMENTAL MUSIC.

' Mr. Jnckings his Belles ' for Harpsichord	**1175**

Instrumental pieces in 2 parts. A number of pieces for Treble and Bass, arranged in Suites, viz. :—29 pieces in G mi: 8 in G ma: 15 in D mi: 6 in D ma: 9 in A mi: 9 in E mi: 19 in C mi: 4 in C ma: 12 in F ma: 10 in B♭ ma. Score **1005**

Bass part only of Almaine, Corrante, Serrabrand and Aire, all being found in 1005 **1022**

Forty-two pieces, Violin part only, nearly all being found in 1005. **599**

Instrumental pieces in 3 parts. A number of pieces for two Trebles and Bass arranged in Suites, viz. : 8 pieces in G mi: 6 in G ma: 15 in D mi, ending in D ma: 4 in D ma: 9 in A mi: 8 in E mi: 9 in C mi: 7 in C ma: 7 in F ma: 9 in B♭ ma. Score **1005**

JENKINS (John).—*continued.*

Bass book of 3-part pieces, of which 59 are found in **1005** : 12 are
not there. Two (Nos. 1 and 2) without name may be by Jenkins
          1011

Sets of pieces a 3 for a Bass, 2 Trebles, Theorbo, and Harpsecord.
4 pieces in D mi. : 4 in D ma. : 4 in G mi. : 4 in B♭ ma. : 4 in
C ma. Thirteen pieces (7 in D mi. : 6 in D ma.) for Bass,
2 Trebles, Lyra Viol, and Harpsecon. Sep.   **1006–9**
Five Almaines for 2 Trebles and Bass. Sep.   **379–81**
Five Phantasias a 3. Sep.   **473–8**
Four sets of Fantasia, Alman and Ayre for Organ, Base viol, and
Treble (Treble and Bass only). Sep.   **777 and 779**

Instrumental pieces in 4 parts.
Twelve Fancies (the last imperfect in Bass book). Sep. **468–72**
    Of these, Nos. 28, 29, 30, and 31 are found sep. **397–400**
        Score **2** ; short score   **436**
    Those numbered 23, 24, 27, 32 are found sep. **473–8**
    That numbered 34, A. and T. only, sep. **716–20**
Two fancies. Sep.   **473–8**
    Of these No. 18, A. and T. only, is in **716–20**
One fancy. Sep. A. and T. only   **716–20**
Ten Aires. Sep.   **517–20**
Forty-nine pieces. Sep.   **367–70**

Instrumental pieces in 5 parts.
Four Fantasias. Sep.   **473–8**
    Of which No. 13 is also Score **2** ; Sep. **403–8**
Two Pavans. Sep.   **423–8**
    Of which the first for Organ is in **1004**

Instrumental pieces in 6 parts.
Four Fantasias. Sep.   **423–8**
    of which those numbered 39 and 40, for Organ, are in **1004**
    and No. 24 is sep. **473–8**
Two Phantasies. Sep.   **473–8**
A set of 4 pieces in C mi. Treble part only **1027**

JOHNSON (Robert), I. A Scottish priest who fled to England before
the Reformation on a charge of heresy. He is called 'peticanon
of Windsore' in **979–83**.

Domine in virtute. 5 v. Sep., wanting Tenor Book **979–83**
Laudes Deo. 2 v. Tr. and Tenor   **982**
Sabatum Maria. 5 v. *Burney.* Sep.   **984–8**
    [After the Canto Fermo part is written 'Tallis : alias Johnson',
which may mean that the copyist was uncertain as to the authorship, or that the Canto Fermo would serve for two settings.]

JOHNSON (Robert), II.   One of the King's Musicians for the Lute,
    1604.   Died, 1634.
  Woodes, rocks and mountains (cf. B.M. Add. MS. 11608). Tr.
    solo   87
  Two Almaines and a Masque tune for Keyed Instrument   1113
        (The Almaine, No. 87, p. 195, is found in the *Fitzwilliam
    Virginal Book*, II, 159.)
  Air for instruments (1 and 2 Treble and Bass). Sep.   379–81
  Two Airs for instruments (1 and 2 Tr., A. and B.) called 'The
    Temporisor' and 'The Wittie Wanton'. Sep.   367–70
  Alman for Lute   532

JONES (   ), ? John.   1728–96. Organist of the Middle Temple,
    Charterhouse, and St. Paul's Cathedral.
  Evening Service in F.   4 v.   Mag. and N. Dim.   Score   762
            Organ part   1229
  Two Chants   1226

JONES (Robert).   Mus. Bac.; Lutenist; fl. 1600–14.
  Singe joyfully.   Full Anthem.   5 v.   Sep., wanting Bass   56–60
  Four Songs from *The Second Booke of Songs and Ayres*, 1601   439
        Arise my thoughts (unfinished).
        Dreams and imaginations.
        Fie what a coyle.
        Now what is love.

JUDD (Edward).   ? end of 17th century.
  Three instrumental pieces, Tr. and Bass, one called 'The Sea-
    man's Dance'   90–1
        (Other pieces in these books may be by Judd.)

KELLY (   ).   ? end of 17th century.
  One Air for Violin, treble only.   362

KELWAY (Thomas).   Organist of Chichester, 1726–47. Died 1749.
  Evening Service in A mi.   4 v.   Mag. and N. Dim.   *Marshall.*
            Score   41
            Organ parts   1225 and (imperfect at beginning) 1228
  Evening Service in B mi.   4 v.   Mag. and N. Dim.   *Rimbault.*
            Score   41
            Organ parts   1225, 1228
  Four chants   1229
        (Of these three are also in 1226, where one is attributed to
    Kent.)

KENT (James).   1700–76.   Organist of Winchester College and
Cathedral.

*All thy works praise thee. V.A. Organ part	**1235**
Bow down thine ear. V.A. Organ part	**1234**
*Hear my prayer. V.A. Organ part	**1228**
*In the beginning. V.A. Organ part	**1228**
*Lord how are they increased. V.A. Organ part	**1235**
*The Lord hath prepared. V.A. Organ part	**1235**
The Lord is my shepherd. V.A. Organ part	**1226**
Psalm Tune (105th Psalm)	**1235**
Single Chant in G mi. (attributed in 1229 to Kelway)	**1226**

(* These Anthems are printed in Kent's *Twelve Anthems*.)

KING (Charles).   Mus. Bac., 1687–1748.   Vicar Choral of St. Paul's.
Service in C.   Te D., Jub., Ky., Creed, Mag., N. Dim.   *Arnold*.

Organ part	**1225**
Kyrie of the same. Organ part	**1231**

Service in F.   Te D., Jub., Mag., N. Dim.   *Arnold*.   Organ part,

wanting end of N. Dim.	**1228**
Organ part with Kyrie and Creed in F.	**1225**

Service in B♮.   Te D., Jub., Cant., D. Mis.   *Arnold*.   Organ

part	**1229**

Sep. voice parts.   Alto (Dec.), wanting beginning of

Te D. ; Tenor and Bass (Dec. and Cant.)	**1220–4**
Single Chant in F	**1226**

KING (Robert).   Mus. Bac.   Musician in Ordinary for the Private
Musick, 1680.   Contributed to song books, 1684–96.   Published
a book of *Songs for One, Two, and Three Voices*.

Air for Violin. Violin part only	**362**
Almand for Harpsichord, by ' R. K.'	**46**

(This is printed among Blow's works, and is probably by him. q. v.)

KING (? Robert, or, perhaps, William.   Born 1624.   Organist of
New College, Oxford.   Died 1680).

Tell me, O tell me, some powers. ' Mr. King.' Song. Bass only	**91**
The Lord is King. ' Mr. King.' V.A. *Cope*. Organ part	**437**
[Out of the horrour. Ps. cxxx. Treble solo. ' Dr. Kinge ', probably author of the words only	**440**]

KIRBYE (George).   Contributed to Este's *Psalter*, 1592, and
Triumphs of Oriana, 1601.   Published Madrigals, 1597.   Died
1633.

Sleepe restles thoughtes. a 4. Sep.	**1074–7, 750–3**
Vayne worlde adiew. a 4. Sep.	**750–3**

KIRBYE (George)—*continued*.

Woe is me my strength fayles. a 4. Sep.   **750-3**
> (These are adaptations to sacred words of 'Sleep now, my Muse', 'Farewell my love', and 'Woe am I my heart dies', from Kirbye's *First Set of English Madrigals*, 1597.)

KREMBERG (James). 'Musician in Ordinary to Her Majesty', i.e. Queen Anne (Eitner).

Aurelia has sweet pleasing charms. 'Compos'd for 1 Bass (voice), 1 Violin or Hautbois, and a Harpsichord or Basson.' Sep. **767**
Lavinia has Majestic charms. Alto Solo with figured Bass **767**
Since I have seen. 'Compos'd for 1 Treble, 1 Flute or Violin, and a Harpsichord.' Sep.   **1067**

LA BARRE. Perhaps Joseph de la Barre, Organist in the Chapel of Louis XIV. Died 1678 (Eitner). There were other composers of the name.

Corant for Harpsichord. 'Labar'   **1236**
Sarabrand   **1177**
> (See also *Bare, Corant*, 1236.)

LAMBE (   ).
'Mr. Lambes Commandments in B♮.' Short Score   **46**

LANGDON (Richard). Mus. Bac. Organist of Exeter, 1753; Ely, 1777; Bristol, 1778; Armagh, 1782. Died 1803.

Lord thou hast been our refuge. V. A. Organ part   **1225**
Not unto us. V. A. Organ part   **1225**
O pray for the peace. V. A. Organ part   **1225**

LANGDON (Tobias). Priest-Vicar, and Sub-chaunter of Exeter Cathedral. Died 1712.

Three catches for 4 v. 'Churchill and Rooke,' 'Goe on great Englands Duke,' 'When a Church,' with autograph letter **1219**

LANGDON (   ).
Three Chants   **1226**

LANIERE (Nicholas). 1588-1666. Master of the Music to Charles I. One of the King's Musicians for the Lutes, 1617-42; and again, 1660.

Amorosa pargoletta. 3 v. A. T. B. Score   **17**
Miser pastorella. 3 v. A. T. B. Score   **17**
Sweet doe not thus destroy me. 3 v. A. T. B. Score   **17**
Two short pieces for instruments (Tr. 1 and 2, and Bass) called 'Symphonia'   **379-81**

LASSUS (Orlandus).   Born at Mons.   Master of the Court Chapel at Munich.   Died 1594.

Angelus ad pastores.   5 v.   Printed in *Sacræ Cantiones*   **984–8**
Dum transisset.   5 v., wanting Tenor book   **979–83**
Susann' vn jour.   5 v. (without words).   *Musica Transalpina*, 1588.
                                                                           984–8
Veni in hortum.   5 v.   *Sacræ Cantiones*   **984–8**
 (See also under *Philips* (*Peter*) for transcription for keyed instrument.)

LAWES (Henry).   1595–1662.   Gentleman of the Chapel Royal.

My song shall be.   V. A.   Organ part with words   **46**
 Sep. A. T. B. Chorus and Tenor verse parts   **1220–4**
 Organ part   **437**
Zadok the preist.   F. A.   Sep. A. T. B. parts only   **1220–4**
 Organ part, without Symphony   **437**
 (For 'Not unto us', adapted by Aldrich from *Zadok the Priest* and Farrant's *Lord for thy tender*, see under *Aldrich*.)
Twenty-four Psalms from Sandys' *Paraphrase upon the Divine Poems*, 1638.   Treble voice and Bass   **365**
 Bass voice   **366**
At dead low ebb of night.   Treble Solo   **350**
Come lovely Phillis. Playford's *Select Musicall Ayres and Dialogues*. Treble voice only   **1114**
I preethee send (cf. B. M. Add. MS. 29386).   Treble voice only   **1114**
While I listen to thy voice.   Bass only   **366**

LAWES (William).   Elder brother of Henry.   Gentleman of the Chapel Royal.   Killed at the siege of Chester, 1645.

Let God arise.   Bass Solo   **18**
The Lord is my light.   V. A.   *Boyce.*   Score   **12**
 Sep. A. T. B. Verse and Chos., T. and B. Chos.
                                                                           1220–4
'Psalmes for 1, 2, and 3 partes to the comon tunes.'   Sep. A. T. B.
                                                                           768–70

The Lamentation. O Lord in Thee.	The humble suite of a sinner. O Lord of whom.
All people that on earth.	The Lamentation of a sinner. O Lord turn not.
Have mercy on vs Lord. Ps. lxvii.	O God my God wherefore. Ps. xxii, Pt. I.
Lord in thy wrath. Ps. vi.	
O Lord consider. Ps. li, Pt. I.	O Lord depart not. Ps. xxii, Pt. II.
Cast me not Lord. Ps. li, Pt. II.	
O God my strength. Ps. xviii.	All yee yt feare him. Ps. xxii, Pt. III.

(Arranged for Verse with Symphonies for Organ, alternating with the common tunes for Chorus.)

LAWES (William)—*continued*.

What if I die for love of thee. Dialogue. Tr. and B. (Cf. B. M.
Add. MS. 11608)   **17**

Instrumental Music.

'Greate Consorte, wherein are Six Setts of Musicke', viz. 7 pieces
in A mi., 6 in C ma., 7 in F ma., 6 in B♭ ma., 18 in D mi., 18
in D ma. Sep. Treble I and II, Theorbo I and II, Bass I
and II   **391–6**
The same, called 'Royall Consorte'   **754–9**
   [The 'Greate Consorte in D mi., 391–6, is identical with the
'Royall Consorte', 754–9, Nos. 1–21, except that Nos. 9, 10,
and 21 of 754–9 are not in 391–6.

   Nos. 22–40 of 754–9 are identical with the set in D ma. in
391–6, except that 754–9 has an 'Eccho', No. 32, not in 391–6.

   Nos. 41–6 of 754–9 are the set in A mi. of 391–6; No. 1 in
391–6 being No. 60 in 754–9 (out of its place).

   Nos. 47–52 are the C ma. set of 391–6, except that No. 9 of
391–6 is only part of No. 47 in 754–9.

   Nos. 53–9 and 61–6 of 754–9 are in the F ma. set and the
B♭ set of 391–6.]
The same sets in D ma., D mi., A mi., and C ma., as in 754–9.
The set in D mi. wants No. 2 (except in the Theorbo Book 483)
and the first 3 pieces in the Bass Books 1 and 2. The set in
D ma. wants No. 22 of 754–9. Sep.   **479–83**
One piece for 3 instruments. Sep.   **379–81**
Three short pieces for 4 instruments. (No. 45 wants Altus and
Tenor; No. 46 wants Cantus and Tenor; No. 44 perhaps be-
longs to the same set.) Sep.   **367–70**
Six pieces for 3 Liero Violls (1st Fantasie, Serabrand, Pauin, Al-
maine, 2nd Fantasie and unnamed piece). Sep.   **725–8**
Organ part of 8 sets, each consisting of Fantazia, Almaine, and Ayre,
 headed 'Mr. Lawes his Organ-part for 2 Violins and a Bass' **430**
Organ part of Instrumental set in 2 parts   **5**
   [The name Will. Lawes is against No. 9, which appears to be
the first movement of a set in G ma. (Nos. 9, 10, 11, and 12) also
found without name in 599 (Treble only). The name W. Lawes
is against No. 16, a piece in D mi., and perhaps No. 15 in D mi.
may also be his, as well as other pieces in the volume.]
The first 12 of these pieces are Nos. 43–54; 17–20 are 55–8
(Treble only) in   **599**
   [The pieces in 599 numbered 43–63 are probably by Lawes.
No. 63 has 'William Laws' at the end.]
Two Almaines, Antick, Corrante, Serrabrand. Bass part only.
                                                                 1022

Allemande for Harpsichord, 'Golden Grove'   **1003**
The Corante and Saraband following are probably by W. Lawes
also.

LAWES (William)—*continued*.

The Almand (The Golden Grove) and Corant to the Golden Grove
(the same as occur in **1003**) **1236**
   [The Golden Grove Almand is printed in *Musick's Handmaid*,
1663.]

LEGRENZI (Giovanni). Born about 1625 at Clusone near Bergamo.
   Maestro di Cappella of St. Mark's, Venice, 1685. Died 1690.

Missa a Cinque Voci con stromenti, in C ma. 'Chirie eleison',
   'Gloria in excelsis', and 'Credo' only. Score **1000**
Songs from *Eteocle e Polinice*, 1680 **945**
      Al suon delle trombe. (Atto 2⁰, Sc. 1.)
      Cieco ognor amante cor. (Atto 3⁰, Sc. 10.)
      Satia pur il tuo furore. (Atto 1⁰, Sc. 21.)
      Su feroci miei Campioni. (Atto 1⁰, Sc. 7.)
      Vibri pur di strali arma. (Atto 1⁰, Sc. 11.)

LE JEUNE (Claude). Born about 1540 at Valenciennes. 'Composi-
   teur de la musique de la chambre du roy' Henri IV. Died soon
   after 1598.

The rocke that Moyses strooke. Pt. I. 4 v. Sep. **750-3**
Those streames of lyuinge water. Pt. II.
The flowing streames of Jordane. Pt. III.
      (Adaptations to English words.)

LEOPARDI (Vincenzo).

Di gia dato. Sopr. Solo **950**

LEVERIDGE (Richard). 1670-1758. Bass singer and song
   writer.

Tell me Belinda, from *The Lady in Fashion*. Treble voice only **389**
Tho' over all mankind, from *Calista*, 1698. Cf. B. M. Add. MS.
   31993. Treble voice only **389**

LOCK (Matthew). Born about 1630 at Exeter. 'Composer in the
   private music', 'for the wind music', and 'for the violin' to
   Charles II. Organist to Catherine of Braganza. Died 1677.

A voice came out of the throne. For two Bass voices and Basso.
   Printed in Playford's *Harmonia Sacra*, Bk. I, 1688.
      Score **43, 48**
How doth the city. V. Anthem. Score **14**
      Organ part, autograph **1219**
Not unto us. V. Anthem. Score **22**
O be joyful (Jubilate). 'A Vers Anthem for Foure Voyces and
   Instruments at Pleasure.' Autograph. Score, with S. A. T. B.
   chos. parts, and 2 Vo., A. and B. String parts inserted loose
      1188

LOCK (Matthew)—*continued*.

O give thanks.   V. A. for 3 part chos. and verse.   Score   **14**
      The same   **1188–9**
      The same with 'Gloria' added.   Aldrich MS.   **12**
      Sep. parts.   Bass complete;   Tenor and Bass, 'Gloria' only   **1220–4**
      Organ (with Gloria)   **1234**
Who shall seperate us.   V. A.   Score   **22**
Agnosce O Christiane.   Bass Solo with Basso.   Printed in *Cantica Sacra* 1674.   Sep.   **623, 625, and 626**
  Bass voice only   **749**
All things their certayne Periods.   New Year's Song for verse and chorus.   Score   **14**
Descende cœlo.   Song for the Oxford Act.   For verse and chorus with Instr. parts, Vo. 1 and 2 and Basso   **619**
In a soft vision.   Song for Tr. solo   **1219**
No musick like that.   'The Firstt songe In yᵉ Empriss off Morocco.' Treble voice only   **692**
The groanes of ghosts.   'A masque sung by vocall musick, beetweene Orpheus, Pluto, Prosserpine, and one woman more, attendantt to Prossepine'.   Score   **692**
When death shall part us.   Dialogue between Thirsis and Dorinda. Treble and Tenor   **49**
      The same for Tenor and Bass   **14, 621**

INSTRUMENTAL MUSIC.

Almand for Harpsichord   **1177**
For 2 parts;   Treble & Bass.   Sep.   **409–10**
    11 sets; 5 pieces in G mi.; 3 pieces in G ma.; 6 pieces in B♭ ma.; 4 pieces in D mi.; 2 pieces in D ma.; 3 pieces in A ma.; 3 pieces in A. mi.; 6 pieces in F ma.; 5 pieces in C mi.; 3 pieces in C ma.; and 6 in E mi.
For 3 parts;   2 Trebles and Bass, with figured Bass.   Score   **8**
    6 sets: 3 pieces in C mi.; 3 in C ma.; 3 in E mi.; 3 in D mi.; 2 in D ma.; 5 in F ma.
For 4 parts.   1 Treble part only   **1066**
    Allman, Corand, Saraband, Gavatt and Air, in D mi.; and 'Mr. Locks Braules in Gamut'. (10 pieces in G mi.; 4 in B♭; 8 in G mi.; 4 in G ma.   Followed by a piece in F ma.)
Mr. Lock's Consort.   2 Trebles, Theorbowe and Bass   **772–6**
      (Only one Treble part; 3 copies of Theorbo part.)
    5 sets; 5 pieces in C ma.; 4 in D mi.; 4 in D ma.; 4 in G mi. (of which the last, a Saraband, is assigned to 'W. G.' as well as to Lock); and 4 in G ma.

LOOSEMORE (? Henry). Mus. Bac. Organist of King's Coll., Cambridge. Died 1670. Or his son George, Organist of Trin. Coll., Cambridge, 1660–82).

LOOSEMORE (? Henry)—*continued*.

Courant for Harpsichord	**1236**
O that mine eyes would melt. V.A. Short Score	**46**

(Cf. B.M. Add. MS. 30932.)

LOWE (Edward). Born at Salisbury about 1610; Organist of Christ Church, Oxford, about 1630; one of the Organists of the Chapel Royal, 1660; Professor of Music at Oxford, 1662. Died 1682.

If the Lord himself. V.A. Sep. S. A. T. Chos. parts; 2 Basses, V. and Chos. **623–6**

Sep. A. and T. Chos.; 1 and 2 Bass, V. and Chos. **1220–4**

O clapp your hands. V.A. Sep. A. T. B. Chos. parts; 1 and 2 Sopr. V. and Chos. **623–6**

Sep. A. T. B. Chos.; B., Verse and Chos. **1220–4**

O give thanks. V.A. Sep. S. A. Chos.; S. T. B., V. and Chos. **623–6**

Sep. A. T. B. Chos.; T. and B., V. and Chos. **1220–4**

O how amiable. V.A. Sep. A. T. B. Chos.; 2 Soprs. V. and Chos. **623–6**

Sep. T., Chos.; A., 1 B., 2 B., V. and Chos. **1220–4**

Sing unto God. A. T. B., Chos.; B., V. and Chos. **1220–4**

Turn thy face face away. A. T. B., Chos. **1220–4**

When the Lord turned. V.A. Sep. A. T. Chos.; 1 and 2 S., B., V. and Chos. **623–6**

Sep. A. T. B. Chos.; B., V. and Chos. **1220–4**

God prosper long. (*Chevy Chase*.) Set for A. A. B. **17**

Sir Eglamore. (The popular song, see *Chappell*.) For S. A. B. Printed in *Pleasant Musical Companion*, Book II, 1687 **17**

The thirsty earth. Setting for S. B., with Chos., S. S. B., of a song for Bass by 'Mr. Roger Hell'. (See *Hill*) **17**

When Death hath snatcht us. Dialogue for S. B. Score **17**

Piece for Harpsichord **1177**

LOYD (   ).

Air for Instruments. Tr. and Bass **362**

LUGGE (John). 'Organist in St. Peters in Exeter.'

Service. Te D., Jub., Ky., Creed, Mag., N. Dim. Organ part **437**

Short Service. a 4. Te D., Bdtus., Ky., Creed, Mag., N. Dim. Organ Score, with words **6**

I am the resurrection. Organ part **437**

Let my complaint. V.A. for Tenor and Bass. Organ part **437**

LUGGE (John)—*continued.*

A collection of organ pieces and voluntaries, each signed John or
    Jo. Lugge.   They appear to be autograph copies   **49**
        Gloria tibi trinitas (6 settings).
        In nomine.
        Miserere (Canon in the 5th).
        Vt re mi fa sol la.
        2 Voluntaries 3 pts.   (The first has passages marked
           'Double', 'Single'.)
        1 Voluntarie 3 and 4 pts.
    An unsigned 'Christe qui lux' in this MS. may be taken to be
    by Lugge.

Mr. Luggs Jigg.   For Harpsichord   **431**

LULLY (Jean-Baptiste).   1633–87.   Generally known in England
    as Baptist or Baptista (q. v.).

Cadmus et Hermionne: Tragedie (1673).   Overture, chaconne and
    other dances, &c.   Score   **23**
            Overture, chaconne from the same.   Score   **1216**
    (An Overture, Gavot, Chaconne, and 2 other pieces, one called
    Les Vents, occur in both MSS.; other pieces are not identical.)

Ritournelles from Thésée (1675); Le Triomphe de l'Amour (1681);
    Persée (1682) with Passacaille from Persée.   Score   **1128**

A collection of songs from Thésée, Voice and Bass only   **95**
        C'estoit dans ces Jardins.
        Reuenez amour.
        Sans une aimable paix.
        Trop heureux qui moissonne.
        Pour les plus fortunés.
        Pretens tu que je sois.
        La valeur à mes yeux.
        Cessez charmante Ægle.
        Faites grace à mon age.
        Doux repos.
        Le depit veut.
        Un tendre engagement.
        Quand on suit.
        N'aymons jamais.
        Sortez ombres.
        Que nos prairies.
        Aymons, tout nous y convie.
        Quel plaisir d'aymer.
        L'amour plaist.
        Ah faut il me vanger.
        Le plus sage s'enflame.

One Violin part of 5 pieces (Baptist), including Overture and un-
    finished Chacon, and a Bourée pour les Egyptiens from Persée,
    and perhaps other pieces by Lully   **1141–2**

LULLY (Jean-Baptiste)—*continued*.
   Piece in Score 'Magicians' (Baptist)   **1141–2**
   Overture in Phaéton (1683). Incomplete score, wanting inner
     parts   **3**
   Ah pour te plaire. Treble Solo. (Sig^{re} Battista)   **17**
   Cessez de vous plaindre. Tr. Solo   **350**
   Sciocca pur tutti. Tr. Solo.   **17, 350**
   See also under *Baptist* or *Babtist* for Violin tunes, and *Batis* (?) for
     Harpsichord music.

LUPO (Joseph). An Italian who was appointed one of Queen Eliza-
   beth's Musicians for the Violins, Nov. 16, 1563. Died 1616.
   Or perhaps Thomas (q. v.) is intended.
   Fancy 'Alte parole' (probably a Madrigal) a 5.
        Organ part   **67**
        Sep. parts (attributed to T. Lupo.)   **527–30 and 1024**

LUPO (Thomas). Probably the 'composer for the Violins' to James I,
   1621, who held his place among the Violins till 1642.
   Have mercy upon me. Anthem a 5, with 2nd Part, For I know-
     ledge my faults. Sep., wanting Bass   **56–60**
   Heare my prayer O Lord. Anthem a 5. Sep., wanting Bass
                       56–60
   Out of the deepe. Anthem a 5. Sep. wanting Bass   **56–60**
   Ay mee can love and bewty. Madrigal a 6. Sep., wanting Bass
                       56–60
   Daphnis came on a soͬmers day. Treble solo   **439**
   Instrumental pieces in 3 parts.
     Fourteen Fantazias. Sep.   **423–8**
     Of these, Nos. 1, 2, 3, 4, 5, 6, 9, 10, 12, 13, 14 are in **401–2**
       (wanting 1st Violin); and Score   **2**
     Nos. 1, 3, 11, 14 are in   **459–62**
     Nos. 9 and 12 (2nd Violin only) are in   **1027**
     Four Phantazias. Sep.   **473–8**
     The same (wanting 1 Violin) **401–2**; and Score   **2**
     Nos. 17 and 19 (2nd Violin only)   **1027**
     One Fancy (besides those above mentioned).
        1st Violin only   **1027**
        2nd Violin and Bass. Sep.   **401–2**
        Score   **2**
     Five (or possibly Six) Fancies not in the former collections.
        Wanting 1st Violin. Sep.   **401–2**
        Score   **2**

   Instrumental pieces in 4 parts.
     Four Fancies for Two Basses and Two Trebles   **716–20**
     Seven Fantazias. Sep.   **423–8**

LUPO (Thomas)—*continued.*

    Of these, Nos. 4, 5, and 7 are in   **473–8**
    One Phantazia (besides those above mentioned)   **473–8**

  Instrumental pieces in 5 parts.
    Eight Fantazias 'for 5 Vyalls to yᵉ Organ'.   Organ   **1004**
          Sep. parts   **403–8, 423–8, 716–20**
          Organ   **436**
    Nos. 1, 2, 6 (end only), 7, 8.   Score   **2**
    No. 5, 6, 8.   Score   **44**
    No. 4.   Organ part   **67**
    Nos. 1, 3, 5.   Sep.   **527–30 and 1024**
    Nos. 2 and 8.   Sep.   **473–8**
    Seven Fancies (in addition to those in **1004**).
          Sep.   **527–30 and 1024**
    (Some are headed 'Miserere', 'O vos omnes,' 'Alte parole,'
      'Ardo' (parts I and II).)
    Of these 'Miserere' and 'O vos omnes' are Score   **2**
          Organ   **436**
          Sep.   **403–8**
    'Alte parole' (ascribed to *Joseph Lupo*, q.v.).   Organ part   **67**
    No. 22 is Score **44**; Organ   **436**
          Sep.   **403–6**
    Two Fancies (besides those in **1004**).   Sep.   **473–8**

  Instrumental pieces a. 6.
    Four Phantazias.   Sep.   **403–8, 473–8**
          Score   **2**
    The first of these in Score   **44**
    Six Fantazias.   Sep.   **403–8, 423–8**
          Score   **2**
    Of these, Nos. 33 and 35 in 423–8 are (Organ part) in   **1004**
    No. 30 and No. 38 (short Score) are in   **436**

M. (D.). [Perhaps Davis Mell.]
    Twelve sets of Tunes, Dances, &c., for instruments.   Treble only
                                                            433

MACQUE (Jean de or Giovanni di).   Published between 1576 and
      1613.   He lived from 1586 in Naples, where he became Master
      of the Royal Chapel.

  My sweet Lais.   Madr. a 5.   The 23rd in Morley's Collection,
      1598.   Score without words   **33**

MALLORIE (   ).   A 16th-century English writer, known by
      a few MS. compositions in the British Museum.

  Miserere a 5.   (Solfa-ing song or instrumental piece, on the Plain
      song.)   **984–8**

MAMMOTT (   ).
Double Chant in B♭   **1143**

MANYARD (John).
Round, 'O follow me Tom, John, and Wilcock'   **358**

MARCELLO (Benedetto). 1686–1739. A Venetian of noble birth,
who held several government posts; chiefly known for his settings
of Paraphrases of 50 Psalms (1724 and 1727).
Hear me when I call. Ps. iv. 2 voices. Score   **1226**
Lord who shall dwell. Ps. xv. V. A. Score   **1225**
O Lord our Governor. Ps. viii. Organ part   **1226**

MARCO or MARC' ANTONIO. See *Cesti*.

MARENZIO (Luca). Died 1599.
Veni Creator. 3 v. Tr., Tr., B. Sep.   **739–43**
(Probably an adaptation.)
Madrigals from *Madrigali a qvatro voci*, 1585, fitted with
English words of a moral or sacred character.
Can any man in country (O bella man). Sep.   **750–3, 1074–7**
Frayle flesh is mortall (Tutto il dì piango). Pt. I. Sep.   **750–3**
Ay me our time (Lasso che pur). Pt. II. Bass only   **753**
How longe Lord (Madonna sua merce). Sep.   **750–3**
The same, 'Fair shepheards queene' from Watson's *Sett of Italian
Madrigalls Englished*, 1590. Score without words   **33**
How ofte oh Lorde (Dolci son le quadrella). Sep.   **750–3**
In darkesome night (Su 'l carro de la mente). Pt. I. Sep. **750–3**
Drawe on bright Day (Vedi ch'egli ama). Pt. II. Sep.   **750–3**
O Lorde my sinnes (Menando un giorno). Sep.   **750–3**
O Lorde view my woefull plighte (Veggo dolce mio bene).
Sep.   **750–3**
The same with other words, 'Oh man view but the flowers.'
Sep.   **750–3, 1074–7**
The same, 'Farewell cruell' from Watson's *Sett of Italian Madri-
galls*, 1590. Score without words   **33**
O who reguardes (Chi vuol udir). Sep.   **750–3, 1074–7**
The holy Angells (Vezzosi augelli). Sep. wanting Treble **751–3**
The same, 'Every singing bird' from Watson's *Sett of Italian
Madrigalls*. Score without words   **33**
Winter is ended (Zefiro torna). Pt. I. Sep.   **750–3, 1074–7**
The same with other words, 'Christe redemptor.' Sep.   **750–3**
The same with other words, 'What shall we render.' Treble only.
740
The same, 'Zephirus breathing,' from Watson's *Sett of Italian
Madrigalls*, 1590. Score without words   **33**
Quousque Domine (Ma per me lasso). Pt. II. Sep.   **750–3**

MARENZIO (Luca)—*continued*.

Di pianti e di sospir. Villanella a 3, from *Il Quinto Libro delle Villanelle*, &c., 1587. Score   55

I must depart (Io partirò). Madrigal a 5 from *Musica Transalpina*, 1588. Organ part without words   67

Madrigals a 5 from Watson's collection, 1590.
       Score without words   33
How long wth vayne complaining (Questa di verd' herbette).
Sweet hart arise (Spuntauan gia).
Sweet singing Amaryllis (Cantaua la più vaga).
When I behold (Venuta era Madonna).
      (All from *Il Primo Libro de Madrigali*, 1590.)
Madrigals a 5 without words, for instruments.
Al lume de le stelle (7th Book of 5 part Madrigals).
       Score   44
A mi Tirsi (7th Book).   Score **2**, organ part   **436**
       Sep.   **403-8**
Arda pur (7th Book).   Score **2**, organ part   **436**
       Sep.   **403-8, 527-30 and 1024**
Caro dolce (3rd Book).   Score **2**, organ parts   **67, 436**
       Sep.   **403-8**
Che se' tu (6th Book).   Score **2**, organ parts   **67, 436**
       Sep.   **403-8**
Deh poi ch' era (7th Book).   Score **2**, organ parts **67, 436**
       Sep.   **403-8**
Ma grideran (7th Book).   Score **2**, organ part   **436**
       Sep.   **403-8**
O doloroso.   Score **2**, organ part   **436**
       Sep.   **403-8**
O disaventura (7th Book).   Score   **44**
Ond' ei di morte (6th Book).   Score **2**, organ parts **67, 436**
       Sep.   **403-8**
Quell' augellin (7th Book).   Score **2**, organ part   **436**
       Sep.   **403-8**
Rimanti in pace (6th Book).   Score **2**, organ part   **436**
       Sep.   **403-8**
Udite lagrimosi (6th Book).   Organ part   67
(See also under *Philips* (*Peter*) for Keyboard Transcriptions.)

MARINI (Francesco Maria).   Chapel master at San Marino; fl. 1637.

Three Motets from *Concerti Spirituali*, 1637. Sep.   **623-6**
     Anima mea.   a 3 (Tr. A. B.)
     Magnum hæreditatis.   a 3 (Tr. A. B.)
     O vos omnes.   a 3.   (A. T. B.)

MARSH (J.), of Chichester.

Six chants   **1143**

MARTINENGO (Gio. Paolo).　Organist of the Cathedral of Pavia, *c.* 1643.

Adoro te for 2 Sopranos or Tenors.　Sep.　　**623–6**
　　　　　(Printed in Casati's *Motela*, 1643.)

MASINI (Antonio).　Maestro di Cappella at the Vatican.　*c.* 1678.

Posso parlar piu.　Cantata for Soprano Solo　　**948**

MASON' (Francesco).　16th-century writer.

Instrumental piece in 4 parts　　**372–6**

MASON (Rev. William).　1724–97.　Canon of York, poet and amateur musician.

Lord of all power and might.　*Page.*　Organ part　　**1226**
Kyrie in D　　**1225**

MELANI (Alessandro).　Maestro di Cappella of S. Petronio, Bologna, 1660 : S. Maria Maggiore, Rome, 1667 : S. Luigi de' Francesi, Rome, 1672 : died 1698.

Te Deum laudamus for 8 voices with Instruments (1 and 2 Trombe, 1 and 2 Violini and Basso), in D ma.　Score　　**85**

MERCURE (John).　Succeeded Robert Dowland as Musician for the Lutes and Voices in Ordinary, 1641 ; died before 1660.

Almaine, Corant and Sarabrand for Harpsichord　　**1236**

MERULA (Tarquinio).　fl. 1615–52.　Maestro di Cappella at Warsaw, Bergamo, and Cremona.

Four Madrigals from *Madrigali* 1623.　Basso only　　**880**
　　Belle ha le perle.
　　Tempesta di dolcezza.
　　Nominativo hic et haec.
　　Nominativo quis vel qui.
　　　　The two last, score　　**1078**
Two Madrigals a 4, from the *Madrigali*, 1624.　Score　　**21**
　　La mia Clori.
　　Immortal Margarita (unfinished.)

MERULO (Claudio), or Claudio da Correggio.　1533–1604.　Organist at St. Mark's, Venice, Mantua, and Parma.

Three pieces for instruments in 4 parts.　Sep.　　**372–6**

MICHAELI (　　　　).　Perhaps Angelo Micheli, one of the Chapel of the Queen of Sweden, Upsala, 1653, who once owned the MS. 377.

Il tempo chi.　Alto Solo.　　**17**

MICO (Richard). A 17th-century writer of instrumental music.

Fancies in 3 parts.
    Seven fancies. Score   **2**
    Sep. wanting 1 Treble   **401–2**
    The first 2 complete. Sep.   **459–62**
    The 3rd and 4th (unfinished). Treble only   **459**

Fancies in 4 parts.
    Seventeen fancies. Sep.   **353–6, 517–20**
    (Two others in 517–20 are probably by Mico also.)

Fancies in 5 parts.
    Fancy headed 'Parte Seconda'. Score   **2, 436**
            Sep. parts   **403–8**
    Two Fantazias. Sep.   **473–8**
    Fantazia and an In Nomine. Sep. **403–8, 527–30** and **1024**
            Short score   **436**
    Pavan. Sep.   **403–8, 423–8, 527–30** and **1024**
            Short score   **436**

MILTON or MELTON (John). *c.* 1563–1647. Father of the poet.
    If ye love me. a 4. Score, without words   **44**
    Three fancies. a 5. Sep.   **423–8**

One Fancy and an In Nomine. a 6. The latter has words for
  2 Treble 'If that a sinner sighs'. (This has no connexion with
  Milton's contribution to Leighton's *Teares*, 1614.) Sep. **423–8**

MISSINO (Gio. Lorenzo). Published a book of Madrigals called
  Tirsi Doglioso at Venice, 1615.

Fifteen Madrigals without words in score, being the contents of
  Tirsi Doglioso, 1615   **21**

Anima del cor mio.   O se vedesti.
Arda pur sempre.   Occhi belli.
Filli dolce ben (Preposta).   Occhi lumi.
Ite caldi sospiri.   Occhi per me.
Lungi da te.   Se l'alm' e in me.
O Donna troppo. Pt. I.   Se 'l miser cor.
S'io vivo. Pt. II.   Tirsi dolce ben (Resposta).
Ma se da voi. Pt. III.

MOCHENI (Francesco) 'in Milano'. A 16th-century writer.
    La gan ba. Piece for instruments a 3   **984–6**

Trinitas in Unitate. Canon a 3 for instruments   **987**

MONFERRATO (D. Natal). Maestro di Cappella at St. Mark's,
  Venice : died 1685.

Two Motets from *Motetti Concertati*, 1660, Libro primo, Opera terza.
Regina cæli, for 2 Tenors. Scores   **20, 621**
         Second Tenor part only   **1178**
Salve Regina for A. T. B. Score   **43**
         Sep.   **623–6**

MONTEVERDE (Claudio). 1567–1643.

Madrigals (without words) from his 3rd and 4th Books.

Cor mio mentre. a 5. 4th Book. Score	21
Cor mio non mori. a 5. Fragment. 4th Book. Score	21
La piaga. a 5. 4th Book. Score	21
La tra'l sangue. a 5. 3rd Book. Score	2
Sep.	404–8, 527–30, and 1024
Short score	67, 436
Luci serene. a 5. 4th Book. Score	44
Sep.	404–8, 527–30, and 1024
Short score	436
O come gran martire. a 5. 3rd Book. Score	2
Sep.	404–8, 527–30, and 1024
Short score	67, 436
Ond'ei di morte. a 5. 3rd Book. Short score	67
Sovra tenere. a 5. 3rd Book. Score	2
Sep.	404–8
Short score	67, 436
Voi pur. a 5. 4th Book. Sep.	404–8
Short score	436
Volgea l'anima. a 5. 4th Book. Score	21

MORGAN (   ). A writer of the end of the 17th century.

Overture and seven pieces for strings. Tenor and Bass only.

351–2

MORLEY (Thomas). 1557–? 1603. Mus. Bac.

SERVICES.

Te D., Btus. Service for verses 'to the Organn'. *Barnard.*	
Sep. A ; T. and B. (Dec. and Cant.) only	1220–4
Organ part	1001

Mag. and N. Dim. 'by minoms': here given as part of the above service. In *Barnard* as a separate Evening Service.

Sep. A. ; T. and B. (Dec. and Cant.) only	1220–4
Organ parts	1001, 1233

Mag. and N. Dim., printed by *Barnard* as part of the verse service above. Sep. A. ; T. and B. (Dec. and Cant.) only 1220–4

Mag. and N. Dim. Organ part 1001

Out of the deep. V. A. *Barnard.*

Sep. Chorus parts, A. T. B. only	1220–4
Organ parts	6, 88
Another organ part with different setting of the verse	6

Two Madrigals a 4, from *Madrigalls to foure Voyces*, 1594, fitted with new words of a moral character.

In sinnes embraces (In dew of Roses)	1074–7
1 and 2 Sopr. only	740, 742
The stately cædare (Besides a Fountain)	750–3

G

MORLEY (Thomas)—*continued*.

Canzonets a 3, from *Canzonets, or Little Short Songs to Three Voyces*, 2nd ed. 1606; fitted with new words of a moral character   **739–43, 750–3**

Angells come flyinge (Cruel you pull away).   1 and 2 Sopr. only   **740 and 742**

Ay mee Lord (Thirsis let some pittie).   2 copies of 1 and 2 Sopr.   **739–43**

Blow sheapheardes (Blow shepherds).   2 copies of Sopr. and Alto   **739–43**

Deep lamenting (Deep lamenting).   2 copies of Sopr. and Alto   **739–43**

Flow O my tears (Doe you not know).   2 copies of 1 and 2 Sopr.   **739–43**

Hold out my hart (Hold out my heart).   2 copies of 1 and 2 Sopr.   **739–43**

How shall a younge man (Love learnes by laughing)   **750–3**

Looke up my soule (Arise, get up).   2 copies of 1 and 2 Sopr., and of Alto (unfinished)   **739–43**

Love not this world (Ladie those eyes).   2 copies of 1 and 2 Sopr.   **739–43**

My thoughts do so delight (Joy, joy doth so arise).   2 copies of 1 and 2 Sopr.   **739–43**

O fly not (O fly not).   2 copies of 1 and 2 Sopr.   **739–43**

O harke, oh harken (Where art thou, wanton).   2 copies of 1 and 2 Sopr.   **739–43**

Oh how my soule (Lady if I).   2 copies of 1 and 2 Sopr.   **739–43**

Oh man why doest (See, see mine owne).   2 copies of 1 Sopr.   **739–43**

O myne eyes (Cease myne eyes).   2 copies of 1 and 2 Sopr.   **739–43**

Remember thy maker (God morrow fair ladies).   1 and 2 Sopr. only   **740 and 742**

This world and all (This Love is but a wanton fit)   **750–3**

What bitter paynes (Now must I dye).   2 copies 1 and 2 Sopr.   **739–43**

When man is dyinge (Farewell disdainfull).   2 copies of 1 and 2 Sopr.   **739–43**

Ye charitable pitty full mynded (Say deere will you not).   2 copies of 1 and 2 Sopr.   **739–43**

Pavine, 'Sacred Ende.'   a 5.   **423–8**

   [The name 'T. Morley' in Cantus part: in Bassus 'Daniell' (? Farrant).   Morley is probably intended.]

MORLEY (William). Mus. Bac.; Gent. of Chapel Royal. Died 1731.

Double chant in D mi.   **1226**

MORNINGTON (Lord). Mus. Doc. ; 1735–81.
Two chants   1226

MOUNTAGUE (H.).   Of the end of the 17th century.
Three instrumental pieces, a 4 ; the last wanting Viola part.
(Three other pieces here are probably his.) Sep.   1183

MUMFORD (   ). *c.* 1700.
Overture and 8 tunes for strings   351–2
   Tenor and Bass parts only.

MUNDY or MUNDIE (John). ' Organist of the kyngs free chappell
of Windsore ', ' sonne of Willm. mundie of the Chappelle gentle-
man '. (Notes in the Part-books, **979–83**.) Mus. Bac., 1586 ;
Mus. Doc., 1624. Died 1630.
Motets, wanting Tenor Book. Sep.   **979–83**
   Edes nostra, a 5.
   In te Domine, a 5.
   Sabbatum Maria, a 6.
   Lamentations, a 5.   De Lamentatione ; Daleth, Juxta
    est ; Lamed, In cuius adventum.
Anthems.   O give thanks. V. A.   Score without words   525
   Score   16
   Sep. parts wanting Bass   56–60
   Bass voice only   1012
   Organ parts   88 (twice), 1230
Verse Anthem wanting the beginning. ? O Lord our Governor
begins ' Thou hast made him lower '. Organ part   6
Lightly she whipped. Madr. a 5 from the *Triumphs of Oriana*, 1601.
   Score without words   33

MUNDY or MUNDIE (William). ' Of the Queenes chapell.' Died
  about 1591.
Motets, wanting Tenor Book. Sep.   **979–83**

Adhæsit pavimento, a 5.	Maria virgo, a 6.
Adolescentulus sum, a 6.	Memor esto, a 5.
Beatus auctor, a 5.	Noli emulari, a 5.
Beatus et sanctus, a 5.	Sive vigilem, a 5.
Beati immaculati, a 5.	The same complete **984–8**
Domine non est, a 6.	Veni creator, a 5.
Domine quis habitabit, a 6.	Videte miraculum, a 5.
Eructavit cor, a 6.	Vox patris, a 6

Fragments of a Magnificat   45
   Et sanctum nomen.
   Qui fecit mihi.
   Sicut locutus.

MUNDY or MUNDIE (William)—*continued*.

O Lord I bow the knees of my heart, a 5. *Barnard.* Sep.,
    wanting Bass   **56–60**
          Sep. A. T. B. only   **1220–4**
          Organ parts   **6, 1001**
          (For alteration by Aldrich, see *Aldrich.*)
O Lorde the maker of all thing, a 4. *Boyce, Barnard*
          Score   **11, 16**
          Sep. A. T. B. only   **1220–4**
          Organ parts   **6, 88, 1001, 1230**
    (In the Index to **16** this is ascribed to H. R. (Henry VIII): in
6 to John Mundy : in **1001** to William.)
O Lord the world's Saviour, a 4. Sep. A. T. B. only   **1220–4**

              SERVICES (ascribed here to William Mundy).
First Service. *Barnard.* Te D., Bdtus., Ky., Creed, Mag., N. Dim.
   Sep. A. T. B. (Dec. and Cant.) only   **1220–4**
          Organ part without Ky. and Creed   **1227**
Short Service. Te D., Bdtus., Mag., N. Dim. Organ part **1227**
          Sep. parts without Mag. and N. Dim. A. T. B. (Dec.
          and Cant.) only   **1220–4**

MUTLOW (William). 1761–1832. Organist of Gloucester.

Unto thee O Lord. V. A. Organ part   **1225**

NANINO (Giovanni Maria). Maestro di Cappella at several churches
    in Rome, and finally at the Sistine Chapel. Died 1607.

My soule shake off. a 3. Sep., with 2 copies of 2 Treble
                                      739–43

NARES (James). 1715–83. Mus. D. Organist of York Minster,
    and of the Chapel Royal.

Single Chant in A   **1226, 1229**

NENNA (Pomponio). Published Madrigals, &c., from 1609 onwards.
    Died before 1618.

Ten Madrigals, in score, without words, from *Il Primo Libro,*
    a 4, 1621   **37**

Ahi dispietata.	O mia luce.
Asciugate i belli occhi.	Ripiglia Ergasto.
Aure liete.	Se gl'occhi.
La mia doglia.	S'io taccio.
Madonna.	Sospir che dal bel petto.

Four Madrigals, in score, without words, from *Il Quinto Libro,*
    a 5, 1603   **21**

Alm' afflitta.	Occhi belli.
Mercè grido.	Tu mi lasci.

NICOLA (   ).
Pieces for Trumpet Solo.   Trumpet part only   731

NORCOME (Daniel).   b. 1576.   Member of the Viceregal Chapel in Brussels.
With Angel's face and brightness. Madr. a 5. From *The Triumphs of Oriana*, 1601.   Score, without words   33

NORRIS (Thomas).   Mus. Bac.   Organist of Ch. Ch. 1776–90.
Hear my prayer.   V. A.   Organ part   1226

NORRIS (   ).   Probably Thomas, q. v.
Three Single Chants   1226

NORRIS (   ).   Probably William.   One of the Children of the Chapel Royal till 1686 ; Master of the Children at Lincoln. Died *c.* 1710.
In Jewry is God known.   V. A.   Score   49

NOUE (   ).   Perhaps Stephen or Simon Nau, both of whom were Musicians to Charles I.
Corant for Harpsichord   1236

OLDRIDGE or ALDERIDG.   See under *Aldrich*.

ORME (Robert).
Advice to a Composer ; 'Gentle artist'. Alto Solo with instrumental Symphonies.   Score   1152
String parts (Vo. 1 and 2, Va., Bass)   1141–2

OTLEY (   ).
Have mercy.   Treble voice part only   598

PALESTRINA (Giovanni Pierluigi da).   Died 1594.
Sixteen Motets, a 4, from *Motecta Festorum totius anni, Liber Primus,* 1571.   Sep.   521–4

Dies sanctificatus.	O Rex gloriæ.
Lapidabant Stephanum.	Loquebantur variis.
Valde honorandus.	Benedicta sit.
Magnum hereditatis.	Lauda Syon.
Tribus miraculis.	Fuit homo.
Hodie Beata virgo.	Tu es pastor.
Ave Maria.	Magnus sanctus.
Jesus junxit se.	Surge propera.

PALESTRINA (Giovanni Pierluigi da)—*continued.*

The whole contents of the 5th Book of Motetts for 5 voices, 1584. Score   10

Lætus Hyperboream. Pt. I.	Surge Petre.
O Patruo pariterque. Pt. II.	Apparuit caro.
Paucitas dierum.	Ecce merces.
Manus tuæ.	Videns secundus.
Tempus est ut revertar.	Rex Melchior.
Nisi abiero.	Ave Regina cœlorum.
Domine secundum.	Gaude gloriosa.
Ave Trinitatis.	Exultate Deo.
Parce mihi. Pt. I.	Tribulationes civitatum. Pt. I.
Peccavi quid faciam. Pt. II.	Peccavimus. Pt. II.
Orietur stella.	Surge Sancte Dei. Pt. I.
Ægypte noli flere.	Ambula Sancte Dei. Pt. II.
Ardens est cor.	Salve Regina.
Sic Deus dilexit.	Eia ergo.

The whole contents of the Book of *Madrigali Spirituali*, a 5, 1594.   Score, without words, excepting the first   8

Figlio immortal.	Santo Altare.
E se mai voci.	Tu di fortezza.
Hor tu sol.	Specchio che fosti.
Dammi scala.	Vello di Gedeon.
E se fur.	Novella aurora.
Dammi vermiglia.	E questo Spirto.
E se 'l pensier.	E dal letto.
Eletta Mirra.	Et arda ogn'hor.
Cedro gentil.	E tua merce.
Fa che con l'acque.	E quella certa.
Se amarissimo.	Anzi se foco.
Horto che sei.	E con i raggi.
E se nel foco.	Regina de le vergini.
Vincitrice de l'empia.	Alfin madre di Dio.
Citta di Dio.	E tu Signor.

[PALLAVICINI (Carlo), fl. 1666 to 1688: a writer chiefly of operas in Dresden and in Venice.

The following songs are found in the libretti of operas set by him, though it is possible that they are not his settings.

Three songs from *Diocletiano.* The words by Matteo Noris were printed at Venice, 1675.

>Basta un guardo.   Atto 1, sc. 4
>Se mi lice baciar.   Atto 1, sc. 17
>Se la piaga sanar potrò.   Atto 2, sc. 6.

PALLAVICINI (Carlo)—*continued*.

Two songs from *Enea in Italia*. The words by Bussani were printed at Venice, 1675.

Chi dice mal d'Amor. Atto 2, sc. 7.
Sei gentile, sei vezzoso. Atto 3, sc. 13.]

PALLAVICINO (Benedetto), of Cremona. Maestro di Cappella to the Duke of Mantua, 1596–1601. Died 1612 or 1613.

Madrigals from the 6th Book of 5-part Madrigals, 1600, without words.

Come vivrò. Score	2
Short score	67, 436
Sep. parts	403–8
Cor mio. Short score	67
Sep. parts	527–30 and 1024
Era l'anima. Score	2
Short score	436
Sep. parts	403–8
O come vaneggiate. Sep. parts	527–30 and 1024

PARSONS (Robert). Gentleman of the Chapel Royal, 1563; drowned in the Trent at Newark, Jan. 1569/70. In the MS. 987 is this couplet :—

Qui tantus primo Parsone in flore fuisti,
Quantus in autumno ni morerere fores !

It has been doubted whether all the works ascribed to Robert Parsons are by this early writer.

Motets (The Tenor Book is wanting in **979–83**).

Ave Maria. a 5	**984–8**
Credo quod Redemptor. a 6. 'Mr. Parsons of the Chapell as some doe say.'	**979–83**
Domine quis habitabit. a 6	**979–83**
Libera me Domine. a 5	**979–83**
Magnificat (extracts only)	**45**

Quia fecit mihi.   a 3.
Sicut erat in principio.   a 4.
Sicut locutus est.   a 4.

O bone Jesu. a 5	**979–83, 984–8**
O quam glorifica. a 3	**45**
Peccantem me. a 5	**979–83**
Retribue servo. a 5	**979–83, 984–8**
Solemnis urgebat. a 6	**979–83**

Services and Anthems.

Deliver me.   a. 6.   *Barnard*.   'Cannon 2 in one in ye unison.'

Sep. parts, wanting Bass	**56–60**
Bass part only	**1012**
Organ parts	**88, 1001**

PARSONS (Robert)—*continued.*

Holy Lord God all mightie. Sep. parts. A. T. B. only   **1220-4**
        Organ part   **1001**
How many hired servants. V. A. Organ part; incomplete. 'Mr. Robert Parsons of Exeter. Anthem of the Prodigall Childe' **6**
Lord comfort those. A. (Verse); T. and B. (Verse and Chos.)
        1220-4
Te Deum, Bdtus., Ky., and Creed. 'His excellent service.' Sep. parts A., T. and B. (Dec. and Cant.)   **1220-4**
        Organ part without Ky. and Creed   **1227**
Enforced by love and feare. a 5. Treble Solo with instruments. *Burney.* Sep. parts   **984-8**

Instrumental Music.

Dela court. a 5. 2 settings. Sep.   **984-8**
Je fili. a 5. Sep.   **984-8**
In nomine. a 5. Sep.   **984-8**
A songe called 'Trumpetts.' a 6, wanting Tenor Book. Sep.
        979-83

PARSONS (William). Contributed to Day's *Psalter*, 1563.
Allmighty God whose kingdom. a 4. 'A prayer for the Kinge.'
        Organ part   **6**
(The name is given here as *William*, but it may be doubted which Parsons is intended.)

PASQUINO or PASQUINI (Bernardo). 1637–1710. Organist of Sta. Maria Maggiore in Rome.
Se l'amare. Aria for Sopr. Solo   **956**

PATRICK (Nathaniel). Organist of Worcester. Said to have died in 1594 (*Mus. Times*, Nov. 1905).
Service for 4 voices. *Arnold* (who ascribes it to *Richard* Patrick). Te D., Bdtus., Ky., Creed, Mag., N. Dim. Scores   **41, 761**
        Organ parts   **1230, 1231**

PEARS (J.)
Nine Chants   **1226**

PECCI (Tomaso). Of Sienna; is said to have died in 1606.
Madrigals a 5 from his First Book, 1602   **510-14**

Ahi che'l mio.	Dolce tormento.
Ahi che spento.	O donna troppo.
Amarillide mia.	Perfidissimo volto.
Cosi in gelida.	Se gl' amorosi.
Cosi pietosa.	

PECCI (Tomaso)—*continued.*

> Madrigals a 5 from his Second Book, 1612   **510–14**

Amor io parto.	Ma che vita.
Che io mora.	O nelle tue.
Del piu leggiadro.	Quel neo.
E pender.	Sospir che del.

PEERSON (Martin). *c.* 1590–1650 or 1651. Mus. Bac. Master of the Children of St. Paul's.

O Lorde in thee. V. A. Sep. parts, wanting Bass   **56–60**

Fantasy, a 5, for instruments. Wanting Alto and Bass. Sep.   **716–20**

Four Fantasies, a 6, called 'Acquaintance', 'Beauty', 'Chowse', 'Delicate'. Sep.   **423–8**

PEETERSEN (John). See under *Sweelinck.*

PEMBRUGE (   ).

Single Chant in F   **1226, 1229**

PEPUSCH (John Christopher). 1667–1752. Mus. Doc. Organist of the Charter House, 1737.

I will magnify. V. A. Organ part   **1111**

O praise the Lord. V. A. Organ part   **1233**

Two Cantatas from *Six English Cantatas.* Vo. 1 part only   **70**
> Fragrant Flora 'The Spring'.
> Miranda.

Songs in *Venus and Adonis* 1715. String parts only (Vo. 1 and 2, Va. and Bass)   **70, 71, 72, 75**

How pleasant is ranging.	Cupid, Cupid, bend thy bow.
Ah sweet Adonis.	Beauty now alone. (Bass only).
With her alone.	Chirping warblers.
Cease your vain.	Thus the brave.
*Wealth is but a slave.	On Love what greater curse.

> * Not printed in *Venus and Adonis.* (? by Pepusch.)

Sonata in F for 2 Flutes and Bass. Sep.   **1141–2**

PERRANDI (G.). Marco Gioseffo Perandi, Kapellmeister at Dresden. Died 1675.

Laudate pueri. a 3. For 1 or 2 Trebles, Bass, and Organs   **1034**

PHILIPS. 'Mr. Philips of the kings privichamber.' (See *Wilder,* *(Philip van).*)

PHILIPS (Peter). Brought up under Sebastian Westcott at St. Paul's.
Published from 1591 onwards; Canon of Soignies and Organist
of the Chapel Royal at Brussels.   Said to have died 1628.

Bow downe thine eare.   a 6.   Wanting Bass.   **56–60**
   (Adapted from 'Cantai mentre' in the First Book of 6-part
   Madrigals, 1596.)
Salve Regina.   a. 6.   Score without words   **21**

INSTRUMENTAL MUSIC.

Pavin, a 6.   'Deo Gratias.'   Sep.   **423–8**
Fantazia, a. 6.   Sep.   **423–8**
Almaine, Corrante and Serrabrand.   Bass only   **1022**

VIRGINAL AND ORGAN MUSIC.

Almande   **1003, 1113**
Deggio dunque partire, Pt. I;   Io partirò, ma il core, Pt. II;   Ma
   voi, Pt. III;   Arrangements of Luca Marenzio's Madrigals in
   Melodia Olympica, 1591   **1113**
*Le Rossignol.   Arrangement of Orlando di Lassos Madrigal in
   Musica Transalpina, 1588   **1113**
*Fece da voi partita.   Arrangement of Philips's Madrigal in the First
   Book of 6-part Madrigals, 1596   **1113**
Benedicam Dominum.   Arrangement   **1113**
Veni creator Spiritus for organ.   By 'P. Phil.'; probably Philips **89**
   * These are also found in the *Fitzwilliam Virginal Book* (I, 288 and 346).

PHILLIPS (Dr.).
Fragment of instrumental piece   **1179**

PIGITT (   ).   Probably Francis Piggett or Piggott, Child of
the Chap. Royal, 1679; Organist of Magd. Coll., Oxford, 1686;
of the Temple, 1688; Chapel Royal, 1695.   Died 1704.

A gigg for harpsichord   **46**
A March for harpsichord (printed in *A Choice Collection of Ayres,*
   1700)   **46**

PICKET (   ).   ? the same as Pigitt (Francis), q. v.
Dialogue between 'Grumpolio and yᵉ witch' (imperfect); and Song
   'Triumphant Musick'   **90–1**
(Apparently inserted in a Scene of Saul and the Witch of Endor.)
Dialogue between Love, Hymen, Time and Fortune.   Tenor and
   Bass voice parts   **90–1**
Tenor voice part   **1211**

PIKE (   ).
'An Antick Tune.'   Bass part only   **91**
Tune for instruments: Treble and Bass   **90–1**

POLWHELE (   ).
Instrumental piece.   Bass part only   **1183**

PORTMAN (Richard).   Organist of Westminster Abbey, 1633.
　Service.   Te D., Btus., Ky., Creed, Mag., and N. Dim.
　　　　　　Score 1002
　　　　　　Bass voice only 1012
　　　　　　Without Ky. and Creed.   Organ part 1227
　　　　　　Mag. and N. Dim. only.   Tenor only 440
　Rejoyce in the Lord.   V. A.   Score 49
　Sarabrand for Harpsichord 1177

PRATT (　　　　).
　Double Chant in D 1226

PRICE (Robert).   A 17th-century writer.
　'Faine I would' for Harpsichord 1236

PRIEST (Nathaniel).   Organist of Bristol in 1724.
　Service in F.   Te D., Jub., Mag., N. Dim.
　　　　　　Score 40
　　　　　　Alto part only 1220
　　　　　　Organ part 1229

PRING (　　　　).
　Double chant in A♮ 1226

PSEUDO-CARISSIMI (? = Aldrich).
　Si linguis hominum for 3 Trebles.   'Jacobi Pseudocarissimi.'
　　　　　　Score 9

PURCELL (Daniel).   Organist of Magd. Coll., Oxford, 1688–95.
　　Died 1717.   Brother of Henry Purcell.
　My God, my God.   V. A. for Treble Solo and Organ accompt.
　　　　　　Score 49
　　　　(A short Chorus is probably missing from the end.)
　O let my mouth.   V. A.   Score 49
　Alas when charming Sylvia's gon.   From 'The Spanish Wives'.
　　Treble voice only; also for Harpsichord 580
　In a grove's forsaken shade.   From 'Amalasont'.   Treble voice
　　only 389
　　　　　　(Both these songs were engraved by Cross.)
　In spight of Despair.   'Song between Hope and Despair.'   Alto
　　and Bass.   Score 1215
　Love I defy thee.   Cantata for Treble Solo, dated 1706/7 1146
　Shepherds tune your pipes.   (Cf. B.M. Add. MS. 31405.)   Treble
　　voice only 360

PURCELL (Edward).   1689–1740.   Organist of St. Margaret's,
　　Westminster.   Son of Henry Purcell.
　Single Chant in G mi. 48
　Single Chant in D mi. 1229

PURCELL (Henry).   Born 1658 or 1659.   Died 1695.

SERVICES AND ANTHEMS.

'First Service in B♮.'   Te D., Btus., Ky., Creed, Mag., and N. Dim.
Score   38
'Second Service in B♮.'   Bdte., Jub., Cant., and D. Mis. Score   38
    Te D., Btus., Cant., D. Mis. of same.   Organ part   1231
Te Deum and Jubilate.   Figured Bass only   440
  (The Te D. and Jub. in D for St. Cecilia's Day, transposed
into C.)
Single Chant in A mi.   Score   48
    Organ   1226 and 1229
Funeral Sentences.   Man that is born : In the midst of life : Thou
know'st Lord.   Score   22
Funeral Sentence written for Queen Mary's Funeral.   a 4.   Thou
knowest Lord, followed by Organ part of the same, and 'The
Queen's Funeral March sounded before her Chariot'.   Score 794
Be merciful unto us.   A. T. B., Verse and Chos.; T. and B., Chos.
only   1220–4
Early O Lord.   For 1–4 voices.   Score   628
In guilty night.   *Harmonia Sacra*, Book II   23
I was glad.   A. T. B., Verse and Chos.; T. and B., Chos. only
                                                              1220–4
    Organ parts   1226, 1235
I will sing unto the Lord.   A. T. B., Verse and Chos. only 1220–4
    Organ part   1230
My song shall be alway.   Scores   22, 766
    (In both written for Bass Solo, not Treble.)
    String parts (1 and 2 Vo., Va., Bass)   1188–9
O all ye people.   a 4.   Score   628
O give thanks.   A. T. B., Verse and Chos. ; T. and B., Chos.
only   1220–4
    Score, without symphonies   1109
    Organ part   1235
O God thou art my God.   Organ part   1232
O God thou hast cast us out.   Organ part   1230
O I'm sick of life.   For 1–3 v.   Score   628
O Lord our Governour.   For 1–4 v.   Score   628
Plung'd in the confines.   'A song' for 3 v.   Score   628
Since God so tender.   For 2 Tenors, Bass and Basso.   Score   628
They that go down to the sea.   Bass Solo and Chos. parts only
                                                              1224
    Tenor Chos. part   1222
    Organ part   1229
When on my sick bed.   For 1–3 v.   Score   628
Beati omnes.   For 1–4 v.   Score   628
Gloria Patri.   a 4.   Score   628
Jehova quam multi.   For 1–5 v.   Score   628

PURCELL (Henry)—*continued.*

ODES, &c.

Celebrate this Festival. Ode for Queen Mary's Birthday. Score (unfinished) to middle of 'Crown yᵉ Altar'.   **23**

     Separate parts (1 and 2 Treble and Bass) to end of 'Kindly treat'   **468–70**

     Kindly treat Maria's Day. Treble Solo   **23**

Hail bright Cecilia. Ode for St. Cecilia's Day, 1692. Score   **32**

     Overture. Score   **1186**

In a deep vision's. Ode for 1–3 voices. Score   **1150**

Raise the voice. Ode for St. Cecilia's Day. Score   **1145**

     Bass part (instr. and chorus)   **470**

OPERAS.

Abdelazer. Overture. Score   **3**

     Aire for Instruments (1 and 2 Treble and Bass)   **363**

Amphitryon. Overture. Score   **3**

Bonduca. Overture. Score   **3**

     Choruses, &c. in Score   **32**

       'Hear us great Rugwith.'

       'Sing divine Andate's praise.'

       'Divine Andate.' Tenor solo.

       'Britons strike home.'

     Britons strike home. Vo. part only   **363**

     Britons strike home, set as Harpsichord piece   **46**

Dioclesian. Overture. Score   **3**

     The '1st Musick'. 2 movements. Score   **1125**

     Chaconne for Flutes in Cañon. Flute parts only   **1183**

     'Sound Fame' and 'Let all rehearse'. 1 and 2 Trumpet parts and Basso   **468–70**

     Country Dance for instruments   **363**

Distress'd Innocence; or, The Princess of Persia. Overture. Score   **3**

Don Quixote. Pt. II. Genius of England. Treble Solo. Voice part only   **360**

Don Quixote. Pt. III. From rosie Bow'rs (opening bars of voice part only)   **360**

Double Dealer. Overture. Score (incomplete)   **3**

     Hornpipe. Parts for instruments   **363**

Fairy Queen. Overture and Second Overture. Score   **3**

     Hornpipe. Parts for instruments   **363**

     O let me weep. Treble solo   **363**

       Bass only   **470**

       End of Violin part   **469**

Gordian Knot Unty'd. Overture. Score   **3**

PURCELL (Henry)—*continued.*

Indian Queen. Overture. Score   **3**
                  Choruses, &c., in Score   **32**

By ancient prophecies.	Wee the spirits.
If these be they.	Greatness clogg'd.
If so your goodness.	Cease to languish.
We come to sing.	While thus we bow.
What flatt'ring noise.	You who at the altar.
Begon curs'd Feinds.	All dismal sounds.

I attempt from Love's sickness. Treble voice part only   **580**
      The same for Harpsichord (unfinished)   **580**
      Treble voice   **389**
I come to sing. Treble voice part only   **580**
      The same for Harpsichord   **580**
Seek not to know. Treble voice, Basso and Hautboy.
    Score without Symphonies   **363**
      Hautboy and Basso only, with Symphonies   **469–70**
Their looks are such. Treble voice part only   **580**
They tell us. Treble voice parts only   **360, 580**
Hornpipe, arranged for Harpsichord   **580**
King Arthur. Overture. Score   **3**
    Come Shepherds. Vo. 1 and 2 and Basso parts   **363**
    Fairest Isle. Treble only without words   **1114**
    Shepherd leave decoying. Fragment of 1 Treble only   **960**
    Sound a parley   **363**
Married Beau. Overture. Score   **3**
Mock Marriage. 'Twas within a furlong of Edinburgh town. Treble voice only   **580**
Oedipus. Choruses, &c., in Score   **32**
    Hear ye sullen powers.
    Musick for awhile.
    Come away: and, Laius hear.
Old Batchelor. Overture. Score   **3**
Oroonoko. Celemene pray tell me. Treble voice only   **389**
Princess of Persia. See Distress'd Innocence.
Rival Sisters. Take not a woman's anger ill. Treble voice only   **580**
Tempest. Dear pretty youth. Treble voice parts only   **580, 960**
Timon of Athens. Choruses in Score   **32**
    Who can resist; and, Come let us agree.
      Overture and nine tunes. Bass only   **482**
      Trumpet overture. Trumpet part only   **1128**
Tyrannick Love. Ah how sweet. Treble voice part only   **580**

PURCELL (Henry)—*continued*.

Virtuous Wife. Overture. Score   **3**
           Overture and 8 Tunes. Va. and Basso only   **351–2**
(The second of these is not in *Ayres for the Theatre*, 1697.)
Thirty tunes in Score from *Ayres for the Theatre*, 1697   **620**

SONGS, &c.

Alas how barbarous. Duett for Treble and Bass. Score   **23**
           (Cf. B.M. Add. MS. 33234.)
From silent Shades. *Orph. Brit.*, Bk. I. Treble Solo   **350**
Lovely Albina. *Orph. Brit.*, Bk. I. Treble voice part only   **580**
Sum up all the delights. Catch. Fragment of Bass only   **358**
Urge me no more. Treble Solo   **350**
Who can behold Florella's charms. *Deliciæ Musicæ*, 1695. Treble
  voice only   **389, 580**

INSTRUMENTAL MUSIC.

Overture and 8 Tunes for strings. Va. and Basso only   **351–2**
Twelve Sonatas of 3 parts in Score   **39**
          (From the Set printed in 1683.)
The same in Score   **1174**
Three 4 part Sonatas in Score   **3**
      (Nos. 7, 8, and 9 of the Set printed in 1697.)
No. 9 of the same (unfinished). Score   **620**
No. 10 of the same. Score   **620**
Fantazia of 5 parts upon one note. Score   **620**
     (The autograph of this is B.M. Add. MS. 30930.)

HARPSICHORD MUSIC.

Saraband from Suite V of *A Choice Collection*, 1696. *Squire*,
  p. 15   **46**
Ground in Gamut. *Squire*, p. 33   **46**
Ground in C mi. *Squire*, p. 39   **1177**
    (Followed by an unnamed movement in triple time also in
  C mi. ? by Purcell.)
Prelude, Allmand, and Corant in G. Suite III of *A Choice
  Collection*. *Squire*, pp. 6 to 9   **1177**
Lesson in A mi. *Squire*, p. 35   **1177**
Air in C. *Squire*, p. 33   **1176, 1179**
Piece in E mi., not in *Squire*   **1179**
Voluntary. *Squire*, p. 35   **1179**
    (Possibly some other Harpsichord pieces in these MSS. may
  be Purcell's.)

PURCELL (Thomas). Gent. of the Chapel Royal, 1660; died
  1682. Uncle to Henry Purcell.
Single chant in G. Score   **48**

PURCELL (Thomas)—*continued.*
Single Chant in G mi. Ascribed to Thomas Purcell or P. Humphries
           1226
        Ascribed to Mr. Purcell   **1229**
Single chant in A   **1229**

PUTTI (   ).
Minuet by Sig{r}. Putti.   Violin part only   **1111**

PYSING (William). Perhaps the same who was Lay Clerk of Canter-
bury Cathedral from as early as 1635 till his death in 1683–4.
The Lord heare thee. V. A.   **61–6**

QUAGLIA (Giovanni Battista). Organist of Sta. Maria Maggiore,
Bergamo ; fl. the 2nd half of the 17th century. (*Eitner.*)
Laudate pueri.   Motet for 3 voices, with instrumental parts.
Score   **1110**

QUINTIANI (Lucrezio), of Cremona.   A Cistercian monk of the
end of the 16th century. (*Eitner.*)
Two Madrigals, a 5.   Dolce esca, Pt. I.; Dolce d'ogni, Pt. II.
Sep.   **510–4**

RADCLIFFE (John).
Eight Chants   **1226**

RAMSAY (Robert). Mus. Bac. Organist of Trin. Coll., Cambridge,
1628–44.
In guilty night. Dialogue for Tr. and Tenor with Basso. Score **18**

RANDALL (John). 1715–99.   Mus. Doc.; Professor of Music in
the University of Cambridge.
Service in D. Te D., Jub., Mag., N. Dim. Organ part **1227**
Evening Service in G. Mag. and N. Dim. Organ part **1227**
Double Chant in D **1226**

RAVENSCROFT (Thomas).   Mus. Bac.; published between 1609
and 1621.
Four Anthems, a 5, wanting Bass   **56–60**
    In Thee oh Lord. V. A.
    Oh let me heare. V. A.
    Oh wofull ruines. Full.
    This is the day when. V. A.

REDFORD (John).   Organist and Master of the Children at St.
Paul's in the 1st half of the 16th century.
Vestri precincti.   Motet a 6, wanting Tenor Book **979–83**
Voluntary for Organ **1034**
Organ pieces named ' Agnus ', ' Miserere ' (two pieces), ' Anguelare
fundamentum ', ' Veni Redemptor ' **371**

REGGIO (Pietro).   Born at Genoa ; settled at Oxford, 1677 ; died, 1685. He published a volume of songs in 1680, from which some of the following are taken.

Miserere mei.   Motet for 2 Trebles and Bass.   Scores   **43, 48**
   [The 3 following are attributed to Reggio in B.M. Catalogue (Add. MS. 31440), but the reasons are not conclusive :—
Cum complerentur. a 4. Basso only   **880**
Jesu dulcissime. a 4. Basso only   **880**
Nigra sum sed formosa. a 4. Basso only   **880**]

SONGS.

Beyond the Art of any Cure.   Treble Solo   **1173**
[Cast Clarissa cast that glass away.   Treble Solo   **1173**
   (Without composer's name, but in a collection of Reggio's songs, to whom it probably belongs.)]
Counsel.   Gently, ah gently Madam.   Treble Solo : printed 1680.   **1173**
Gold. A mighty pain to love it is.   Treble Solo : printed 1680   **46**
The Judgement. Wake sleeping ones.   Treble Solo   **1173**
      Wanting last page   **865**
Know Celia since.   Treble Solo   **17**
Quando l'alma.   For Tr. and Bass : printed 1680   **17**
The Swallow.   Foolish Prater : printed 1680   **46**

ROBERTS (John).
Saraband for Harpsichord   **1003**
Almain, unnamed piece and Jigg for Harpsichord   **1177**
Coranto and unnamed piece for Harpsichord   **1236**

ROBINSON (John).   Organist of Westminster Abbey, 1727–62.
Double Chant in D   **1226**

ROGERS (Benjamin).   1614–98.   Organist of Magdalen College, Oxford, 1664–85 ; Mus. Doc. 1669.
Service in D. *Boyce*, &c. Te D., Jub., Ky., Creed, Mag., N. Dim.
      Score   **41**
The same, with Sanctus. Bass only   **1012**
The same, with Sanctus. Organ parts   **1225, 1231**
The same, without Creed. Short Score   **46**
The same, without Mag. and N. Dim. Tenor only   **440**
Evening Service in G. Mag. and N. Dim. 1666. Printed by *Rimbault* under the name of Peter Rogers. Bass only   **1012**
      Organ part   **1227**
Evening short service altogether in A re key. a 4. *Rimbault.* Autograph Score, 1684. Mag. and N. Dim.   **21**
Te Deum patrem colimus. a 4. 'This hymn is song every day in Magdalen College Hall, Oxon, Dinner, and Supper, throught

H

ROGERS (Benjamin)—*continued.*

the yeare, for the after Grace, by the Chaplains, Clerks, and Choristers there.' Autograph Score, 1685 — **21**

Behold now praise. *Boyce.* Bass only — **1012**

      Organ parts — **1230, 1235**

Bow down thine ear. V. A. Autograph Score, 1677, February 13. — **21**

How long. *Cope.* Bass only — **1012**

      Organ part — **1235**

I beheld and lo. 'Hymnus Apocalypticus.' V. A. Autograph Score, 1678 — **21**

I will magnify thee. V. A. Tr. 1 and 2, A. T. B., Verse and Chos. — **623–5**

O pray for the peace. F. A. a 4. *Cope.* Score — **11**

      Bass only — **1012**

      Organ parts — **1230, 1235**

O that the salvation. a 4. *Cope.* Autograph Score, 1684 — **21**

Rejoice in the Lord. Bass only — **1012**

Teach me O Lord. *Boyce.* Organ part — **1228**

INSTRUMENTAL MUSIC.

Preludium, Aire, Aire, Eccho, Saraband, 'Windsor Chase,' in D ma. (and perhaps the following, Aire, Corant, and Saraband in D ma.). Bass only — **1011**

Corant, Corant (La sedois), Sarabrand, unnamed piece, Corant, Sarabrand, Gigue, for Harpsichord — **1236**

ROGIER (   ).

Onse Vader in Hemel-ryck, for Lute — **1014**

RORE (Cipriano de). *c.* 1516–65. Chapel Master of St. Mark's, Venice, and of Parma.

Two fancies in 5 parts. Sep. — **372–6**

ROSENMÜLLER (Johann). Born *c.* 1619. Organist at Leipzig, 1651–5. Capellmeister at Wolfenbüttel, 1674–84.

Miserere mei. Motet for 3 voices with accompt. for 2 violins.

      Score — **764**

      Bass voice and Organo — **687**

Turris fortissima. Motet for 3 Trebles, with accompt. for 2 Fagotti and Organo. Score without words — **764**

ROSINGRAVE (Daniel). Organist successively of Gloucester, Winchester, Salisbury, and St. Patrick's, Dublin. Died 1727.

Lord thou art become. F. Anthem for 5 voices. Score — **1215**

ROSSETER (Philip). Lutenist. Published *A Booke of Ayres,* 1601; *Lessons for Consort,* 1609. Died 1623.

Sweete come againe. Treble voice and Bass. From *Ayres,* 1601 — **439**

ROSSI (Luigi).   Born at Naples.   Died 1653.

MOTETS.

Domine quinque talenta. a 4. (S. S. B. B.) Score   83
Exulta, jubila. a 2. (S. S.) Score   83
Peccantem me. a 3. (T. T. T.) Score   83
Summi regis. a 2. (S. S.) Score   83

CANTATAS, &c., FOR TREBLE SOLO, UNLESS OTHERWISE STATED.

A chi lasso   **17, 350**
Adorate mie catene   947
Al far del dì. a 3 (S. S. T.)   996
Amanti ardire. a 3 (S. A. B.)   377, 996
Amanti piangete   951
Amor, se devo. a 2 (S. A.)   377, 996
Ancor vive una   947
Anime voi che   350, 950
A piu sventure   947
A te mio core. a 2 (S. A.)   996
C'è altra pena   948
Che sventura   949
Con incerta speranza   949
Con rauco mormorio   951
Cor dolente. a 4 (S. A. T. B.)   996
Credei col gir lontano   946
Datemi pace. a 2 (S. S.)   996
Deh perche. a 3 (S. A. B.)   996
Del silentio   952
(Printed in The Musical Antiquary, July 1911.)
Di desir. a 3 (S. A. B)   996
Dite o cieli. a 2 (S. and B.)   377
Dolenti pensier. a 3 (S. A. B.)   996
E che cantar   949
Erminia sventurata (here attributed to Carissimi, but see *Wotquenne*)
     946

E si crede   951
Fanciulla son io   17
Ferma il piè   946
Filli mia   947
Fra le pene   947
Furie d'Averno   946
Gionto il fatale dì   950
Hor ch'in notturna. a 3 (S. A. B.)   996
Hor che fra l'ombre. a 4 (S. S. S. B.)   996
Hor che l'oscura   946
Ho voto di non   947
Il contento. a 2 (S. S.)   996

H 2

SANCES (Giovanni Felice)—*continued.*

    Deus in adjutorium.   S. and Bass.

        Scores   **43** (beginning only), **49, 1178**

        Sep.   **623–6**

    Domine ne memineris.   Two Sopranos.   Score   **49, 1178**

        Sep.   **623–6**

    Dulcis amor.   Bass Solo.   Scores   **43, 48, 1151**

    Judica me.   Two Sopranos.   Scores   **49, 1178**

        Sep.   **623–6**

    Lætamini in Domino.   Soprano Solo.   Scores   **43, 48, 49**

    Laudemus viros.   Two Tenors.   Scores   **49, 1178**

    Magnificemus.   S. S. Bass.   Sep.   **623–6**

    O crux benedicta.   A. T. B.   Sep.   **623–6**

    O Domine guttæ.   A. T. B.   Sep.   **623–6**

    O Jesu mi dulcissime.   S. S. A. B.   Sep.   **623–6**

        Bass only   **880**

    O quam speciosa.   Alto Solo.   Score   **49**

    Plagæ Tuæ.   A. T. B.   Sep.   **623–6**

    Psallite Domino.   Two Sopranos.   Sep.   **623–6**

    Quemadmodum desiderat.   Alto Solo.   Score   **49**

    Solvatur lingua.   Tenor Solo.   Score   **49**

    Tota pulchra es.   Alto and Tenor.   Scores   **49, 1178**

        Sep.   **623–6**

    Vulnerasti cor.   S. and Tenor.   Sep.   **623–6**

SAVAGE (   ).

    Single Chant in C   **1226**

SAVERY (John).

    Te D. and Jub. in C.   Organ and voice parts. (Tr. A. T. B., Dec. and Cant.)   Sep.   **1202**

    Teach me O Lord.   V. A.   Organ and voice parts. (Tr. A. T. B., Dec. and Cant.)   Sep.   **1202**

SAVILE (Jeremy).   Of the middle of the 17th century.

    Fa la, without words.   Tr. and B. only   **598**

SAVIONI (Mario), of Rome.   Singer in the Papal Choir from 1642. Published in 1660, 1676, &c.

    Ten Cantatas for Soprano Solo   **998**

Augellin che non.	Maggio torna.
Entro lo spatio.	Ohimè Madre.
Fuora del' mio Regno.	Oue scorre.
Il tuo sonno.	Se l'amar.
Io pur ti dissi.	Volete altro.

SCARLATTI (Alessandro). 1659–1725.

Operas (I). Scores.

Il Flavio Cuniberto.   Vocal and Instrumental parts.   Score   **989**
Gerone Tiranno di Siracusa, 1692.   MS. written 1693.   Score
990
La Teodora Augusta.   Score **991**

Operas (II). Separate Songs.

L'Aldimiro ovvero Favore per Favore, 1687.
   Songs arranged for Soprano Solo with Basso. **955**
     Chi l'alma m' ha tolta (also in 954). (Cf. B.M. Add. MS. 31506.)
     Due vaghe pupille (also in 954).   (Cf. B.M. Add. MS. 31506.)
     Io non so se potrai fingere.   Printed in *Thirty-six Arietta's.
     c.* 1753.
     Se di Tisbe hauro la sorte.   (Cf. B.M. Add. MS. 31506.)
     Voglio amar chi mi disprezza.   (Cf. B.M. Harley, 1265.)
     Printed in *Thirty-six Arietta's.*
[The following are found in the libretto of *L'Aldimiro*, but no complete score of the music seems to exist with which to collate them **955**
     Amor vuolle cosi.
     Chi t'intende O nume alato.
     Del tuo cor tempri le pene.
     È fanciullo il Dio.
     È uanto crudele d'un alma.
     Fantasmi orribili di gelosia.
     Foglio lieve in cui (also in 954).
     Forti Heroi la cui fè sol.
     Fù guerriero.
     Impiagami, tormentami (also in 954).
     Piante voi.
     Questa destra che maestra (also in 954).
     Se il ciel vi concedesse.
     Se pena s'inventa che avanzi.
     Se tù credi che verace.
     Sentirsi lo dare è un gusto.
     Spade ultrici.
     Spirto eccelso il cui valore (also in 954).
     Tanto basti per farmi morire (also in 954).
     Tra le straggi e le contese.
     Un alma che amando.
     Un vezzo, un guardo (also in 954).]
Dal Male il Bene, 1687.   Songs arranged for Soprano Solo and
   Basso : collated with the Berlin Score.
     Apri le luci amanti.   (Printed in *Thirty-six Arietta's*)   **955**
     La gioia verace favella nel cor. (Cf. B.M. Harley, 1265)   **955**

SCARLATTI (Alessandro)—*continued*.

    S' Ape amante io giungo à suggere   **954**
        (Originally Tenor Aria in B♭.)
    Tu ferito da miei sguardi   **955**
[A setting of the words 'Diro il ver ma diro poco', found in the libretto, is not identical with the setting in the Berlin MS.]

Il Pompeo. 1683-4-8. Two Songs arranged for Soprano Solo with Basso   **955**

    Lusingami speranza (also in 954).
    Tormentosa gelosia.

Gli Equivoci in Amore ovvero La Rosaura 1690.

    Non dar piu pene O caro, arranged for Soprano Solo with Basso. (Cf. B.M. Add. MS. 31506)   **954**

[The following songs are found in the libretto of *Flavio*, 1688, but none of the music is known to exist elsewhere, with which to collate them.

Nineteen Songs arranged for Soprano Solo and Basso   **957**

    Ad altri in braccio.
    Al mormorio del pianto.
    Ardo penando.
    Chi l'impero hà su gl'affetti.
    Chi vuole innamorarsi.
    Cosi mi basta per non morir.
    E in dubbio il core s'un bacio.
    In amor son fortunata.
    In quel volto.
    Mio cor che sara con l'arco.
    Non so amar chi non mi piace.
    Nò, non viver penando.
    Ogni stella ch' in Ciel ruota.
    Partite, abbandonatemi.
    Risorta la speme.
    Scherza, ride, festeggia si.
    Se nel soglio io poso il pie.
    Spera mio cor chi sa.
    Vengo a voi piaggie latine.]

[The following songs are found in the libretto of *La Rosmene ovvero L'Infedeltà Fedele*, 1688.

Ten songs from *Rosmene* arranged for Soprano Solo with Basso   **957**

    Amare è fingere di non amar.
    Col freddo tuo velen ritorna.
    Come cede la porpora all' oro.
    Fiumicel ch' hor presto hor lento.
    Lampo d'or che in istante.
    O quanto hai da soffrir.
    Perche amor vedea languire.
    Se misero oggetto d'affanni.

SCARLATTI (Alessandro)—*continued*.

    Son ferito e tu sei quell' arciera.

    Spoglia esangue in marmi.

Four songs from *Rosmene* arranged for Soprano Solo with Basso

          954

    Amor seconda il bel desir.

    Di morir già non pauenta.

    Già che Amor non fu bastante.

    Se versasti da tuoi lumi.]

Serenata. 'Venere, Adone, Amore.' Serenata. a 3 v. con strom^ti e due Trombe. Score   **992**

CANTATAS, ARIETTAS, &c., FOR SOPRANO SOLO.

A voi che l'accendeste. (*Dent*)   **993**

Al fine ò Clori amata. (*Dent*)   **993**

Aure, io son. (*Dent*)   **993**

Come potesti   **993**

Deh per mercè. (*Dent*)   **993**

    [This Cantata is elsewhere ascribed to Astorga.]

Dov' è Filli   **993**

Lontan' dal idol mio. (*Dent*)   **993**

Reggie Paludi, addio. (*Dent*)   **958**

Tanto strano. (*Dent*)   **993**

    [Cara e dolce libertà, **958**, is printed as Scarlatti's in *Thirty-six Arietta's*, London, *c.* 1753. It is printed as Cesti's by Pignani in 1679 and should be assigned to him. A version of it as a Duet is printed by Hawkins, 1776 (IV, 94) as Cesti's.]

SEVERO DA LUCCA (Antonio), fl. at the end of the 17th century.

CANTATAS FOR SOPRANO SOLO.

Desiri partite   **956**

Pensieri tacete   **956**

Senti pur l'alma   **956**

Sù la spiaggia   **956**

Vieni ò mia cara   **954, 956**

SHENTON (Richard).

Cantate Domino and Deus Misereatur in D, Organ part   **1231**

SHEPHERD or SHEPPERDE (John). Magister Choristarum and Organist at Magdalen College, Oxford, 1542. Supplicated for the Degree of Mus. Doc. 1554. He is here called ' of the Chappelle,' an appointment not recorded elsewhere. (See 979–83.)

O God be mercifull vnto us. a 4. Organ part.   **6**

    MOTETS. &c. (The set **979–83** is imperfect, wanting the Tenor Book.)

Adesto nunc. a 6. Sep.   **979–83**

Beata quoque. a 5.   **979–83**

SHEPHERD or SHEPPERDE (John)—*continued*.

Beati omnes. a 5	979–83
Beatus auctor. a 8	979–83
Cetus omnes. a 5	979–83
Confitebor tibi. a 5	979–83
Cor vestrum (2 settings). a 6	979–83
Deo nostro. a 5, 'for men'. Entered twice	979–83
(As the parts are interchanged, this motet is complete.)	
Deus misereatur. a 5	979–83
Dilectissima. a 6	979–83
Esurientes implevit. a 5. (From a Magnificat.) *Burney*. Sep.	984–8
Et insulæ munera offerent. a 6	979–83
Fecerunt unanimes. a 5	979–83
Funde preces. a 5	979–83
Hec dies quam. a 6	979–83
Hic nempe mundi (2 settings). a 5	979–83
Hierusalem. a 6	979–83
Ibant magi. a 6	979–83
Ignis vibrante. a 7	979–83
In perpetuum. a 5	979–83
Judica me. a 5	979–83
Laudes Deo for 2 Tenors	45
Media vita. a 6	979–83
Noctis recolitur. a 8	979–83
Procedens a throno. a 5	979–83
Procedens a throno. a 6	979–83
Quia fecit mihi. a 4. (From a *Magnificat*)	45
Sabbatum Maria (2 settings). a 6	979–83
Salva nos (2 settings). a 7	979–83
Scandens tribunal. a 5	979–83
Sicut erat. a 3. (Probably from *Magnificat*)	45
Sicut locutus. a 4. (From a *Magnificat*)	45
Solemnis urgebat. a 6	979–83
Sumens illud. a 6	979–83
Te celorum (2 settings). a 6	979–83
Te eternum. a 6. (From a *Te Deum*)	979–83
Tu fabricator. a 6	979–83
Tui precatus. a 6	979–83
Verbum caro. a 6	979–83
Virgo cunctas. a 6	979–83

SHERLY (   ).

Pavin and Gallard for Lute	439

SIMMES (William).   Of the early 17th century.

Awake fond thoughts. a 6 (wanting Bass)	56–60
Rise oh my soule. V. A. a 5 (wanting Bass)	56–60
Seven Phantazias. a 5 (Nos. 34–40). Sep.	716–20
The last of these (No. 40) for Organ	67

SIMONE (Pier). Late 17th century.
Dimmi O Ciel. Aria for Treble Solo　　　　　956

SIMPSON or SYMPSON (Christopher). A 17th-century viol
player, and writer on music. Died 1669.
Bass part of 26 pieces in suites, against the last of which is
Mr. Sympson's name　　　　　1021
Treble part of 21 pieces, against the last of which is Mr. Sympson's
name　　　　　1027
(Probably all are by Simpson.)
Two Grounds in C for instruments. Bass and Ground only　1183

SMITH (Robert). Said to have been one of Capt. Cooke's first set
of Chapel Royal boys, 1660. Words of Anthems by him are in
Clifford. A Robert Smyth was Musician in Ordinary for the
Lute, 1673, till his death in 1675. (See *The King's Musick.*)
O Time thy wings. A Dialoug between Philander, Time, and
Death. a 3. Score　　　　　23

Instrumental Music.
Four short pieces in B♭. Treble and Bass　　　　　90–1
Seven tunes for violin. Treble only　　　　　362
Eleven tunes (or perhaps sets of tunes). Treble only　　361
Sixty-one pieces for 2 Violins and Bass, wanting 1st violin, including
50 unnamed pieces, 2 Gavots, 1 Almaine, 5 Corantoes, 1 Jigg,
1 Saraband, and 1 Ground　　　　　1025–7
Brawls, &c., for strings, including　　　　　1183
    (i) Ground in B♭. (also in 1025–7) for 2 Violins and Bass.
    (ii) Chaconne in B♭. 1 Violin only.
    (iii) 'Mr. Rob. Smith's Brawls in De sol re.' 5 Tunes (3 in
        D ma., 2 in C ma.) for 2 Violins and Bass.
    (iv) Tunes 'made in Oxford'. 1 Violin only, of which 3
        are in F ma. (including Minett and Jigg) and 3 in A ma.
    (v) 'Mr. Smith in C fa utt', 6 tunes; and 2 in D mi. for 1
        and 2 Violins, Va., and Bass. The 2 Violin and Va.
        parts wanting for No. 5 in C.
    (vi) Four tunes in G mi. and 2 in B♭ for 1 and 2 Violins,
        Va. and Bass.
Piece for Harpsichord　　　　　1003

SMITH (　　　)? Robert.
Two single Chants. a 4. Score　　　　　48

SORIANO (Francesco). Born at Rome, 1549. Chapel Master in
several churches at Rome; head of the Choir of St. Peter's, 1603.
Died about 1621.
Ye prysenors poore lifte up your hartes. a 3.　　　1074–7

SOUPER (　　　).
Double Chant in A　　　　　1226

SPENCER (J.)
Two Double Chants   **1226**

SPENCER (William). His name is on the fly-leaf of **361**, as owner (?).
One tune for Violin.   Treble only   **362**
Perhaps William Spencer is the 'W. Sp.', whose name is given as composer to songs from Charles Davenant's *Circe*. Treble and Bass instrumental parts only   **90–1**
    Come every Demon.
    Lovers who to their.
    [' Last night when all the Village slept' (Bass only) may also be from *Circe*, and the following which have no composer's initials (Bass only):
    Young Phaon.
    Maids in wishes.
    Piece without words.]

SPONTANO (Bartolomeo). Probably Spontoni is intended. Chapel Master of the Cathedral of Verona.   Died after 1588.
O my sad soule.   2 parts only   **740** and **742**

SPORTONINO ? (Marc'Antonio). If this name is correctly deciphered, it is otherwise unknown.
Doue uai pensier.   Cantata for Soprano   **946**
Pensier che uoi.   Cantata for Soprano   **951**

STAGGINS (Nicholas). Mus. Doc. Master of the King's Band, 1682; first Professor of Music at Cambridge.   Died 1705.
Two tunes for violin.   Treble only   **361**
One tune for violin.   Treble only   **362**

STANLEY (Charles John). Mus. Bac. Born 1713. A distinguished blind Organist.   Master of the King's Band, 1779.   Died 1786.
My strength.   V. A.   Organ part in D   **1233**
        Fragment of opening solo transposed to F   **22**

STOKES (Thomas).
The Stocking.   Cantata, begins ' Sylvia whose eyes'.   (Printed in the 18th century.)   **1111**

STONARD (William). Mus. Bac. Oxon., 1608.   Organist at Christ Church.   Died 1630.
Magnificat and Nunc Dimittis in D.   Organ part   **1227**

STONE (John).
' Hye Landers March' for Harpsichord   **1175**

STRABRIDGE (John). A 16th-century writer.
Sabatum Maria.   Motet a 5 (wanting Tenor Book)   **979–83**

STRADELLA (Alessandro).   Born about 1645.   Died 1682.
MOTET.
Benedictus Dominus.   a 2.   (S. A.).   Score   **1206**
CANTATAS.
Ardo, sospiro.   a 2.   (S. B.)   **997**
Chi hauesse.   Soprano Solo   **948**
Da Filinda.   Soprano Solo   **948**
Figli del mio cordoglio.   Sopr. Solo   **952**
Fulmini quanto.   a 2.   (S. B.)   **997**
La ragion m'assicura.   a 2.   (S. B.), with Instruments.   Score **48**
Quando mai ui stancherete.   Sopr. Solo   **952**
Sopra un' eccelsa.   Bass solo   **48**
    (Elsewhere called *Il Nerone*.   Printed by Lonsdale, edited by Molique.)

STRIGGIO (Alessandro).   Born at Mantua about 1535; in the service of Cosmo de' Medici at Florence.   Died at Mantua in 1587.
'Il Ciccaláméto di Donne.'   a 7   **1155–61**

Pt. I.   Nella uaga stagion.   a 4. | Pt. III.   Ho udito.   a 7.
Pt. II.   Bvon giorno belle donne.   a 7. | Pt. IV.   Il Gentilhuom.   a 7.
  | Pt. V.   Orsu stendiamo.   a 7.

    From *Il Cicalamento delle Donne al Bvcato, et la Caccia di Alessandro Striggio* [&c.], Venice, 1567.

STROGERS (Nicholas) or Strowgers.
Esurientes implevit.   a 3.   (S. S. B.) }
Sicut locutus est.   a 2.   (S. B.) }   **45**
    (Fragments of a Magnificat.)
Non me vincat.   a 5   **984–8**
Service.   a 4.   *Barnard.*   Venite (Bass only), Te D., Ben., Ky., Creed, Magn., and N. Dim.   Organ part   **1001**
      Without Venite.   Score, without words   **1002**
      Organ part   **6**
      Te D., Ben., Mag., and N. Dim. only.   Organ   **1227**
A doleful deadly pang.   Soprano Solo, with accompt. for instruments.   a 5.   Sep.   **984–8**
Three In Nomine's.   a 5.   Sep.   **984–8**
Two In Nomine's and a piece 'vpon ut re my fa soul la' for Organ
                           371
    (The name is difficult to read against the 2 In Nomine's, and is not certain.)

STROUD (Charles).   Born about 1705.   Child of Chapel Royal; Organist of Whitehall Chapel.   Died 1726.
Hear my prayer O Lord.   *Page.*   A. T. B. only.   Sep.   **1220–4**
      Organ part   **1229**

STUBBS (Simon).   A contributor to Ravenscroft's *Psalter*, 1621.
  Father of Love.   a 5.   Bass wanting   56–60

SWEELINCK (Jan Pieterszoon).   Born 1562.   Organist at Amsterdam.
    Died 1621.
  Fantasia aℓs discantus super vt re mi fa sol la   1113
            The end part (wanting beginning) also in   1003
    (This is printed on p. 25 of the Organ music, vol. i of the
  Collected Works; also found in the *Fitzwilliam Virginal Book*,
  ii. 26.)

TALLIS (Thomas).   'Organiste of the queenes chappelle.'   'Mortuus
    est 23 Nouembris.   1585.   Sepultus Grenouici in Choro Ecclesiæ
    parochialis,' is written in 984–8.   An earlier entry in the same
    set is :—' Talis es et tantus Tallisi musicus, vt si fata senē auferrent
    musica muta foret'; also elsewhere :—'Tallisius magno dignus
    honore senex.'

Motets, &c.

    (The set 979–83 wants the Tenor Book.   The Motets marked
  with an asterisk are printed in *Cantiones quae ab argumento sacrae
  vocantur . . .* 1575.)

Adesto nunc.   a 5.   979–83
De lamentacione.   a 5   979–83
Domine quis.   a 5   979–83
*Facti sunt Nazaræi.   a 5   984–8
Gaude gloriosa.   a 6   979–83
            The 3-part opening of the same   45
Hec deum celi.   a 5   979–83
Incipit lamentacio.   a 5   979–83
*In manus tuas.   a 5.   Score (unfinished), without words   10
Laudate Dominum.   a 5   979–83
Magnificat (*Et exultavit*).   a 5   979–83
Miraculum videte.   a 6   979–83
*O sacrum convivium.   a 5   984–8
            (See *I call and cry*.)

O salutaris.   a 5   984–8
Quidam fecit.   a 6   979–83
*Sabbatum dum transisset.   a 5   979–83
*Salvator mundi.   a 5   984–8, 10
*Salvator mundi.   a 5 (another)   984–8, 10
Salve intemerata.   a 5   979–83
Solemnis urgebat.   a 5   979–83
Tu fabricator.   a 5   979–83
Variis linguis.   a 7   979–83
    [A 'Sabbatum Maria' is ascribed to 'Tallis alias Johnson' in
  the Tenor book with the plain song part, 987.   In 984 and 985,
  to Johnson (I), q. v.]

TALLIS (Thomas)—*continued.*

SERVICES, &C.

Morning and Evening Service. 'First Service.' a 4. *Barnard, Boyce,* &c. Te D., Btus., Ky., Creed, Mag., N. Dim. Score **1002**
      Short Score without words **525**
      Tenor voice only **440**
      Organ **437, 438, 1001**
The same with Sanctus inserted on slips. Sep. A. T. B. only
  1220–4
The same with Sanctus. Organ parts **88, 1231**
The same with Venite and Offertory Sentence, 'Not every one.' Organ **6**
Sanctus of same. Organ **437**
      Tenor only **440**
The same. Unfinished Score (beginning of Te D. only) **9**
Te Deum (F). a 5. Organ part **1001**
Single Chant **1226**
Preces and Psalms and Responces. *Barnard.* Sep. A. T. B. (Cant. and Dec.) **1220–4**
      Bass Decani only **1148**
(The Psalms are :—
    (1) Ps. cxix. Second Part. Wher with all shall a young man.
    (2) Ps. cxix. Third part. O doe well unto thy servant.
    (3) Ps. cxix. Fourth part. My soul cleaueth.)
(The Preces and Responses are in Jebb i, 141–2.)
Preces and Responses. Organ part (without inner parts) as in Lowe's *Short Direction,* 1661 **437**
Preces with Venite, Responses, and Litany. a 4. Score **48**
  'Mr. Thomas Tallis his Litany-service, For men.'
  'No need of a second Countertenor, if there be boys to sing his part 8 notes higher.'
      (Jebb i, 21, 25.)
Preces, Psalm tune, Responses, a 4 ; Litany, a 5. Score **9**
      (Jebb i, 33, 46.)
Preces, Responses, Latter Suffrages and Litany. Single voice part
  1015
Litany. a 5. Sep. **510–15**
    (Agrees in the main with **9**, but not altogether.)
Litany. Sep. A. (imperfect) T. B. only **1220–4**
(Not in Jebb ; agrees in the main with **9**, but not in Alto voice.)
Litany. Organ part. **88**

ANTHEMS, &C.

All people that on earth. Full Anthem. Sep. A. T. B. only **1220–4**
All people that on earth. For Aldrich's adaptation see under *Aldrich.*

TALLIS (Thomas)—*continued*.

Blessed be thy name. a 5. *Barnard*. Organ   **1001**
    (Adapted from *Mihi autem nimis* in *Cantiones*, 1575.)
Come Holy Ghost. (Veni Creator). *Parish Choir*. Sep. A. and
    B. only   **1220–4**
        Organ part   **1229**
Discumfit them O Lord. a 5. Organ   **1001**
    (Adapted from *Absterge Domine* in *Cantiones*, 1575.)
I call and cry. a 5. *Barnard*, &c. Sep. A. (imperfect), T. B.
    only   **1220–4**
        Short Score without words   **525**
        Score   **11**
        Organ parts   **6, 15, 47, 88, 1001, 1230, 1234**
    (Adapted from *O sacrum convivium*, q. v.)
I look for the Lord. a 5. See under *Aldrich*.
If ye love me. a 4. *Day*, 1560 and 1565, &c. Organ   **6**
O thou God allmightie. a 4. Organ   **1001**
Out from the depe. a 4. Organ   **6**
Teach me thy way. Organ   **1001**
With all our hearts. a 5. *Barnard*. Score   **11**
        Short Score without words   **525**
        Organ parts   **47, 1230**
    (Adapted from *Salvator mundi*, No. I, q.v.)

Instrumental.

Two pieces for the Organ. 'Gloria tibi Trinitas ij parts on a rownd
    tyme'; and an unnamed piece.   **371**
Unnamed piece   **1034**

TAVERNER (John). 'Of cardinall wolsayes chappell who died at
    bostone and there lieth.' 'Homo memorabilis.' (Notes in **981**
    and **983**.) Master of the Children of Cardinal College, Oxford.
    (N.B.—The set **979–83** is imperfect, wanting the Tenor Book.)

Mass. a 6. 'Gloria tibi Trinitas'   **979–83**
Te Deum. a 5.   **979–83**
Fragments of a Magnificat   **45**
    Esurientes implevit. a 4.
    Et semini ejus. a 4.
    Quia fecit mihi. a 4.
    Sicut erat. a 3.
    Sicut locutus. a 3.
Ave dei. a 5   **979–83**
Christe Jesu. a 5   **979–83**
Dum transisset. a 5   **979–83, 984–8**
Ecce mater. a 2   **982**
Gaude plurimum. a 5   **979–83**
Mater Christi. a 5   **979–83**

TAVERNER (John)—*continued*.

O splendor gloriae.   a 5   **979–83**
     (The second part of this is by Dr Tye.)
Sabbatum Maria.   a 5   **979–83**
Traditum militibus.   a 3   **45**

INSTRUMENTAL MUSIC.

Quemadmodum.   a 6 (without words)   **979–83**
In Nomine for Organ   **371**

TAYLER or TAILER (   ).   A 16th-century writer ; perhaps
John Tayler, Master of the Children of Westminster.   *c.* 1562.
Christus resurgens.   a 6   **984–8**

TAYLOR (C.).   Perhaps Charles, who contributed to Henry Play-
ford's *Theatre of Music* (1685).
Cantate Jehovæ for 2 Sopr. and Bass.   Sep.   **623–6**

TAYLOR (Daniel).   There was a singing-man of Westminster of
this name in 1625 (see *The King's Musick*).   Buried April 1643
(*Westminster Abbey Registers*).
Sing wee merely.   Anthem a 6.   Bass part only   **1219**
Appollo did in musick's art.   Alto voice part   **1219**

TAYLOR (Miss E.).   Pupil of Crotch, Organist of Kingston.
Seven chants   **1143**

TAYLOR (John).   Son of Robert T., whom he succeeded as Musician
for the Viols and Voices in 1637.   (See *The King's Musick*.)
Aire ; Aire, Almaine and Serrabrand in C.   Bass part only   **1022**

TAYLOR (Robert).   Musician for the Lutes and Voices to Charles I.
Died 1637. (See *The King's Musick*.) Perhaps the same as Robert
Tailour, who published *Fifti Select Psalms of David* in 1615.
Goe my flocke.   Treble Solo   **439**
I never laid me down.   Treble Solo   **439**
Two Almaines for Three Liero Violls.   Sep.   **725–8**

TENAGLIA (Antonio Francesco).   A Florentine, who lived in Rome :
see *Eitner*.
Non diamo in barzellette.   Soprano Solo   **947**

THORNOWITZ (Henry).
Almande, Courante, Menuet, Air Amor, Air Cross, for Harpsichord
                                               1142

TOLLETT or TALLETT (perhaps Thomas).
Mr. Tallett's Tunes in the Play call'd *The Cheats, or the Canting Astrolleger*; for strings. a 4. Vo. 1 and 2, Va., Bass. Overture, Bore, Horn-Pipe, Scotch Tune, Aire, Entre, Jigg, Chacone. Sep.   **944**
(Probably John Wilson's Comedy, *The Cheats*, written 1662.)
Mr. Tollett's Tunes. a 4. Va. and Bass parts only. (1) Overture and 6 tunes. (2) Overture and 9 tunes. Sep.   **351–2**

TOLLIT (George). A George Tollet contributed to Playford's *Division Violin*, 1685. One of the name appears among the Dublin City Music in 1669. (See *Int. Mus. Ges., Sammelbände* 1909–10, p. 33.)
Tunes, &c., for Strings. a 4 (Vo. 1 and 2, Va., Bass)   **1183**
(The name or initials of George Tollit appear on the pieces numbered 10, 12, 13, 18, 30; but others are probably by him.)
Ground in D for strings. Vo. 1 and Bass only   **1183**

TOLLIT (Thomas). This name appears in the Dublin City Music in 1669, 1678, 1688. One of the King's musicians 1693 to 1696 (*The King's Musick*). Published (with John Lenton) *A Consort of Musick in three parts*, 1694; and wrote *Directions to play on the French Flageolet*.
Tunes for strings. a 4 (Vo. 1 and 2, Va. and Bass)   **1183**
(The Va. part is missing to No. 28, and from 31 to end.)
The name or initials of Thomas Tollit appear on the pieces numbered 19, 20, 21, 22, 31, 38, 41, 50, 51, 55; but others are probably by him, as these pieces seem to be often arranged in suites.)

TOMASI (Biasio), of Comachio, in the Roman States, where he was organist in 1611 and 1615.
Motets, a 4, from *Motecta*, opus sextum, 1635. Basso continuo only   **880**
Kyrie (Lettanie B. V.).
O Maria.
Quasi cedrus.

TOMKINS (Thomas). Mus. Bac., 1607; Organist of Worcester Cathedral and of the Chapel Royal, 1621. Died 1656.
Service in C. The First Service printed in *Musica Deo Sacra*, 1668. Venite (T. and B. only). Sep.   **1220–4**
Mag. and N. Dim. Organ part   **88**
The same transposed into G. Te D., Btus., Mag., N. Dim., Ky., Creed. Organ part   **437**

TOMKINS (Thomas)—*continued*.

Service in D. a 4. The Second Service printed in *Musica Deo Sacra*. Te D., Jub., Ky., Creed, Mag., and N. Dim. Score
    1002

The same, without Ky. and **Creed.** Organ part   **1227**

ANTHEMS.

Those marked * are printed in *Musica Deo Sacra*, 1668.

*Above the stars. V. A. Sep. A. T. B. only   **1220–4**

*Blessed be the Lord. V. A. Sep. A. T. B (1 and 2) only **1220–4**

Deere Lord of life. a 6. Sep.   **61–6**

It is my well beloved's voice. a 6. Treble voice part only, incomplete   **62**

Know you not. 'Prince Henry his Funerall Anthem.' Cantus only   **61**

        Organ part   **702**

        Voice parts. Treble (unfinished), **698**; Tenor **700**

             2 Contra Tenor (unfinished), **704**; Bass **706**

*O Lord let me know. V. A. Sep. A. T. B. only   **1220–4**

*Thou art my King. V. A. Sep. A. T. B (1 and 2) only **1220–4**

        Organ part (2 versions)   **6**

        Organ part   **1001**

*O pray for the peace. V. A. Sep. A. T. B (1 and 2) only **1220–4**

Four pieces for Virginal. Pavan, Almaine, and two unnamed pieces (59 and 61)   **1113**

    (The Pavan is found in *The Fitzwilliam Virginal Book*, ii, 51.)

TRABATONE (Egidio). Organist of St. Vittore in Varese; fl. 1628–38.

Motets a 4 from *Concerti a 2, 3, e 4 Voci*, Libro Secondo, 1629. Basso continuo only   **880**

    Dicite nobis.

    In celis hodie.

    Kyrie eleison (Lit. B. V. Mariæ).

    Lætis nunc mentibus.

    Laudate Dominum.

    Qui habitatis.

TRAVERS (John). Organist of the Chapel Royal. Died 1758.

Single Chant in E   **1226, 1229**

TRESURE (Jonas).

Five pieces for Harpsichord   **1236**

    (1 unnamed, 2 Courants, Courant 'variola', Ayre.)

TUCKER (Rev. William). Priest and Gent. of Chapel Royal, and Minor Canon and Precentor of Westminster, 1660. Died 1679

O give thanks. a 5. *Page.* Short score, without words   **525**

        Bass part only (twice entered, once 'false')   **1012**

        Sep. parts. A. T. B. only   **1220–4**

I 2

TURNER (William). 1651–1740. Chorister of Ch. Ch. Oxford ; afterwards Child and Gentleman of the Chapel Royal. Mus. Doc. 1696.

Thus mortals must submit. Sopr. Solo. Printed in *Harmonia Sacra*, 1688   **350**

Air (Treble and Bass, without words)   **1154**

Sixteen Single Chants and one Double Chant   **49**
(The 16th is the single chant in A generally given to H. Purcell.)

Four Single Chants (3 of them are in **49** and one in **1229**)   **48**

Two chants (one of which is Turner's First in **48**)   **1229**

Two chants doubtfully ascribed to Turner   **1226**
(One is by Aldrich ; the other, 'alias Green', is printed as H. Purcell's by Hullah, and in the *Parish Choir*.)

TWIST (John).   One of the Musicians in Ordinary for the Violin, 1671–87.

Twelve short pieces for instruments. 1 Violin part only   **1183**

TYE (Christopher). Mus. Doc. Organist of Ely. Died 1572/3.

Motets, &c.
(The Set **979–83** is imperfect, wanting the Tenor Book.)

Ad te clamamus exules. a 5   **984–8**

Ave caput. a 3. (Part of a longer work)   **45**

Cantate Domino. a 6   **979–83**

Et cum pro nobis. a 5.   Pt. II of Taverner's *O Splendor gloriæ*, q. v.   **979–83**

Miserere mei Deus. a 5   **979–83**

Omnes gentes. a 5   **984–8**

Peccavimus. a 7   **979–83**

Quæsumus omnipotens. a 6   **979–83**

Quia fecit mihi. a 4. (From a Magnificat)   **45**

Tellus flumina. a 3. (Part of a longer work)   **45**

Unde nostris. a 4. (From a longer work)   **45**

Anthems, &c.

Blessed are all they. a 4. Organ part   **6**

Christe rising. Pt. I
Christe is risen. Pt. II } a 6. Sep., wanting Bass   **56–60**

Giue almes. a 4. Organ part   **88**

Haste thee O God. a 4. Printed by *Barnard*, &c., as by Shepherd. Organ parts   **6, 88**

I lifte my hearte. a 5. *Barnard*. Sep., wanting Bass   **56–60**

I will exalt thee. Pt. I
Sing unto the Lord. Pt. II } a 4. *Barnard*, &c. Score   **48**
Organ part   **1230**

TYE (Christopher)—*continued*.

O God be mercifull.   a 4.   *Barnard*.   Organ part   **6**
Save me O God.   a 4.   Organ part   **6**
To Father Sonne and Holy Ghoste.   a 5.   Sep., wanting Bass
56–60

INSTRUMENTAL MUSIC, IN NOMINES, &c.

Ascendo.   a 5   **984–8**
In Nomine.   a 5   **984–8**
Madonna.   a 5   **984–8**
  The same, for organ   **371**
Rubum quem.   a 5   **984–8**

VALLET (Nicholas).   A French lutenist; settled in Amsterdam about 1614.

Tanneken.   a 2.   (Instrumental piece)   **1013–5**

VECCHI (Orazio), of Modena.   Born *c.* 1551.   Chapel Master at Modena, 1596.   Died 1605

Clorinda.   Madrigal a 5.   Without words.   Sep.   **404–8**
  Score   **2**
  Short scores   **67, 436**
    (Clorind' hai vinto, from *Madrigali a cinque voci*, Libro primo, 1589.)
Do not tremble.   Madrigal a 5, from Morley's *Collection*, 1598. Score without words   **33**
      (Tremolauan le frondi, from *Madrigali*, 1589.)
The white delightfull swanne.   Madrigal a 5, from Yonge's *Musica Transalpina*, 1597.   Score, without words   **33**
      (Il bianco e dolce cigno, from *Madrigali*, 1589.)

VENOSA (Carlo Gesualdo, Prince of).   Born in the middle of the 16th century ; still living in 1613.

Madrigals a 5, from the Prince of Venosa's First Four Sets of 5-part Madrigals.   Sep.   **510–4**

(3) Ahi dispietata.	(1) Hai rotto e.
(1) All' apparir.	(3) Languisco e moro.
(2) Baci soaui.	(4) Mentre gira.
(1) Candida man.	(2) Mentre Madonna (Pt. I).
(1) Caro amoroso.	(2) Ahi troppo (Pt. II).
(1) Che sentir.	(4) Moro e mentre (Pt. I).
(3) Deh se già.	(4) Quando ed lui (Pt. II).
(3) Del bel de bei.	(1) Non mi togl' il.
(3) Dolcissimo sospiro.	(4) Questa crudele.
(4) Ecco morirò (Pt. I).	(4) Sparge la morte.
(4) Ahi già mi discoloro (Pt. II).	

Madrigal a 5.   Beltà poi che.   From the 6th Set of Madrigals a 5. Score, without words   **21**

VENOSA (Carlo Gesualdo, Prince of)—*continued*.

The Basso Continuo part of the Pr. of Venosa's 5-part Madrigals,
Books I, II, and IV.   Without words   **880**

Book I.

Caro amoroso.	O mio soave ardore.
Ma se tal'.	Sento che nel.
Hai rotto, e.	Non è questa.
Se per lieve.	Ne tien face.
Che sentir.	Candida man.
In piu leggiadro.	Da l'odorate spoglie.
Se cosi dolc' è 'l.	E quell' Arpa.
Ma s'averrà.	Non mai non.
Se taccio.	All' apparir.
O com' è gran.	Non mi togl' il.

Book II.

Baci soavi.	O dolce mio.
Quant hà.	Tirsi morir.
Madonna io.	Frenò Tirsi.
Com' esser può.	Mentre mia.
Gel' hà Madonna.	Non mirare.
Mentre Madonna.	Questi leggiadri.
Ahi troppo.	Felice primavera.
Se da si nobil.	Danzan.
Amor pace.	Son si belle.
Si gioioso.	Bell' angioletta.

Book IV.

Luci serene.	Moro e mentre.
Tall' hor.	Quando di lui.
Io tacero.	Mentre gira.
In van dunque.	A voi mentre.
Che fai meco.	Ecco moriro.
Questa crudele.	Ahi già mi.
Hor ch' in gioia.	Arde il mio cor.
O sempre crud'.	Se chiudete.
Cor mio deh.	Il sol qual' hor.
Dunque non.	Volgi mia luce.
Sparge la morte.	

VENTURI (Stefano).   Published between 1592 and 1598.

As Mopsus went.   Madrigal a 5.   From Morley's *Collection*, 1598.
   Score without words   **33**

VICARY (   ).

Single Chant in A   **1226**

VINCENTI (Alessandro), of the second half of the 17th century.

Io mi sento. Cantata a 2 for 2 Sopr.	**14**
Vano è il desio. Cantata a 2 for 2 Sopr.	**14**

(The first has the name in pencil only.)

VINCENTIO (   ).   This may be the 'master composer' whom Pepys heard in London in February 1666/7.   ? The same as the above.

Voglio amarvi luci.   Song for Sopr.   **350**

VIOLINO (Carlo del).   See under *Carlo.*

VITALI (Angelo), of Modena.   A writer of the second half of the 17th century.

Confitebor tibi.   Motet for 3 v. (2 Trebles and Bass), with parts for ' 2 violini, 2 viollette, e violone '.   Score   **765**

W. (M.)

Seventeen Chants   **1226**

WALKLEY (here also spelt Wakeley), probably Anthony Walkley, 1672–1717.   Organist of Salisbury.

Service in F.   Te D., Jub., Sctus., Ky., Creed, Mag., N. Dim.

Sep. A. T. B. only	**1220–4**
Organ part	**1229**
The same, without Sctus., Ky., and Creed. Organ	**1232**

WALOND (William).   An Oxford organist who took his Degree of Mus. Bac. in 1757 from Ch. Ch.   Or else, perhaps, the organist of Chichester, 1794–1801, died 1836, who may have been son to the former.

Cantate Domino and Deus misereatur in E♭.   Organ part   **1228**

WARD (John).   Published a Set of Madrigals in 1613, dedicated to Sir Henry Fanshawe, to whose household he was attached.

ANTHEMS.

How longe wilt thou forgett. V. A. a 5, Bass wanting	**56–60**
Let God arise. V. A. a 5 (for 2 Basses). *Barnard.* 2 copies, one transposed. Sep.	**61–6**
Sep., wanting one Bass	**56–60**
Sep. A. T. B. (1 and 2) only	**1220–4**
Organ parts	**6** (unfinished), **67**
Praise the Lord O my soule, O Lord. V. A. a 6 (for 2 Basses). Wanting one Bass. Sep.	**56–60**

WARD (John)—*continued.*

Praise the Lord O my soul and all.   V. A.   Ps. ciii in 5 portions;
  a 3 (S. A. B.).   Sep.   **61–4–6**
                    Organ parts   **67, 1215**
                    (1) Praise the Lord.
                    (2) The Lord executeth righteousness.
                    (3) For looke how high.
                    (4) The daies of man.
                    (5) The Lord hath prepared.

MADRIGALS AND SACRED PART-SONGS.

Cruell unkinde. a 5.   Wanting Bass   **56–60**
Downe caytive wretch.   Pt. I }
Prayer is an endlesse.   Pt. II } a 5.   Wanting Bass **56–60**
Downe in a dale. a 5.   Wanting Bass   **56–60**
If heav'ns iust wrathe.   'Passions on the death of Sr. Hen.
  Fanshawe.' a 6.   Wanting Bass   **56–60**
My breast I'le sett. a 5.   Wanting Bass   **56–60**
No obiecte dearer.   'Passions on the death of Prince Henry.'
          a 6   **61–6**
          Wanting Bass   **56–60**
          Organ part   **67**
This is a joyfull, happy holy day.   (On the birth of a Prince.) a 6.
  Wanting Bass   **56–60**
Well sounding pipes.   Pt. I. }
As sharps and flats.   Pt. II. } a 6.   Wanting Bass **56–60**

INSTRUMENTAL PIECES.

Fancies a 4.   Six Fancies a 4.   Sep.   **459–62, 397–400**
          Score   **2**
          Organ part   **436**
     The 1st and 2nd also in **473–8**; the 5th, 4th, and 2nd are
  also in **517–20**; the 6th in **423–8**.
Fancies a 5.   Eleven Fancies a 5.   **468–72**
Of these the 1st, 3rd, 9th, and 11th are in Score in   **44**
The 10th is in **473–8**.
All but the 8th.   Sep. in **404–8**; in Score in **2**; and Organ
  part   **436**
Fancy a 5, called 'Cor mio'.   Sep.   **423–8, 473–8, 404–8**
          Score, **2**; Organ part   **67, 436**
Fancies a 6.   Nine Fancies and 2 In Nomines a 6.   Sep. **423–8**
Of these the Fancies numbered 6, 7, 8, 10, 11, and 29, and the
  2 In Nomines are also Score   **2**; sep. **404–8**
          Fancy No. 29 and In Nomines 12 and 13.   Organ
          part   **436**
          In Nomine 13.   Sep.   **473–8**
          Fancies.   No. 7 and 29.   Score   **44**

WARROCK or WARWICK (Thomas).   Organist of Chapel Royal,
   1625; and Musician for the Virginall up to Lady Day, 1642.

I lifte myne eyes.   Anthem a 5.   Wanting Bass.   Sep.   56–60
Oh God of my salvation.   Anthem a 5.   Wanting Bass.   Sep.
                                                        56–60

WATTON (Robert).

Single Chant for *Venite*   437
Another Single Chant   437

WEBB (R.).   Perhaps the Rev. Richard Webb, Minor Canon of St.
   Paul's, 1808.

Two Chants   1226

WEBSTER (Maurice).   Musician to James I and Charles I.   Died
   1635.   Compositions by him are printed in Thomas Simpson's
   Taffel Consort, Hamburg, 1621.

An Eccho (in 3 parts) for 2 Trebles and Bass.   a 3.   Sep.
                                                        379–81
   Another Setting of this Eccho, sep.   367–70
Pauan and 3 Almaines.   a 4   367–70

WEELKES (Thomas).   Mus. Bac.   Organist of Winchester College
   and of Chichester.   Died 1623.

Alleluiah I heard a voyce.   Salvation and glory.   F. Anthem a 5.
   Wanting Bass   56–60
         (This is often catalogued as Alleluiah, Salvation.)
Gloria in excelsis Deo, synge my soule to God the Lorde.   F.
   Anthem a 6.   Wanting Bass.   Sep.   56–60
Hosanna to the sonne.   F. A. a 6.   Wanting Bass.   Sep.   56–60
Lorde to thee.   F. A. a 5.   Wanting Bass.   Sep.   56–60
Oh Jonathan.   F. A. a 6.   Wanting Bass.   Sep.   56–60
O Lord God almightie.   F. A.   A. T. B. only   1220–4
         Organ part   1001
O Lord grant the kinge.   *Barnard.*   Organ part   1001
         Bass voice part only   1012
When David heard, Pt. I.   } F. A. a 6.   *Mus. Ant. Soc.*
Oh my sonne Absalom, Pt. II. }
         Sep., wanting Bass   56–60
Te Deum and Jubilate.   a 4.   Organ part   437
Magnificat for Verse and Chorus.   Organ part   88
The Kery and Creed.   Organ part   88

WEELKES (Thomas)—*continued.*

Fourteen Ballets and Madrigals, a 5, from the collection printed in 1598.   Score without words   **33**

Give me my heart.
Say daintie dames.
Phillis goe take thy pleasure.
In pride of May.
Now is the bridals.
Sing Shepherds after me.
Lady your eye.
We shepherds sing.
I love and have my love regarded.
Come clap thy hands.   Pt. I.
Phillis hath sworn.   Pt. II.
Farewell my joy.
Now is my Cloris.
Unto our flocks.

The whole contents of Weelkes's ' Madrigals of 5 and 6 parts ', 1600. Score without words   **33**

Ten Madrigals of 5 parts.
Cold winter's Ice.
Now let us make.
Take heere my heart.
O care thou wilt (Pt. I).
Hence care, thou art (Pt. II).
See where the maides.
Why are you Ladyes.   Pt. I.
Harke, harke, I heare.   Pt. II.
Lady the birds.
As wanton birds.

Ten Madrigals of 6 parts.
Like two proud armies.
When Thoralis delights.
What have the gods (Pt. I).
Mee thinkes I heare (Pt. II).
Three times a day.
Mars in a furie.
Thule the period (Pt. I).
The Andalusian Merchant (Pt. II).
A Sparow hauck proud.
Noell, adew.

From *Ayeres or Phantasticke Spirites* (1608), here written for Single Voice   **439**

Fower armes, to neckes.
Ha ha this world doth pass.
Late in my rash accountinge.
The nightingale.

From *Madrigals to 3, 4, 5, and 6 Voyces*, 1597, with new words.
The greedy wretch. a 3. (Cease sorrows now.)
    Sep.   **739, 741, 743**
The worldly man. a 4. (Our country swains.) Sep. **1074–7**

WELDON (John). 1676–1736.   Organist of New College, Oxford. and of the Chapel Royal.

Hear my crying. *Boyce.* Organ part   **1230**
In thee O Lord. *Boyce.* Organ parts   **1230, 1234**
*I will lift up mine eyes. *Page.* Organ part   **1233**
O how pleasant. Treble voice part only   **683**
        Organ part   **1235**

* Printed in Weldon's *Divine Harmony, Six Select Anthems.*

WELDON (John)—*continued.*

†O Lord rebuke me not.   Organ part   **1235**
*O praise God in his holiness.   *Parish Choir.*   Organ parts, **1226**;
  twice in **1230**.
*O praise the Lord.   *Parish Choir.*   Organ part   **1226, 1230**
†Thou art my portion.   Organ part   **1233**
The wakeful nightingale.   Tr. voice only.   (Engraved by Cross,
  c. 1700)   **389**
'A sett of tunes' in D mi.   Overture, Minuet, Almain, Corant, and
  Canon 'Two in one on a ground'.   Sep. Instr. parts.   1 and
  2 Violin, Bass   **479, 480, 482**

> * Printed in Playford's *Divine Companion*, 1701.
> † Printed in Weldon's *Divine Harmony, Six Select Anthems.*

WERT (Giacches de).   *c.* 1536–96.   Maestro di Cappella at Mantua.
Like flowers we spring.   S. and A. only   **740, 742**

WHYTBROOKE.   A contributor to Day's *Certain Notes*, 1560.
'Hugh Ashton's Maske.'   a 4, wanting Bass   **979–83**
  Probably a composition on this ground by Whytbrooke whose
  name is attached to the contra tenor part.

WHYTE or WHITE (Robert).   Organist successively of Ely, Chester,
  and Westminster Abbey.   Died 1574.

Motets.

Ad te levavi.   a 6.   Sep., wanting Tenor   **979–83**
Appropinquet deprecatio.   a 5.   Sep.   **984–8**
Deus misereatur.   a 6.   Sep., wanting Tenor   **979–83**
Domine quis habitabit.   Three settings.   a 6.   Sep., wanting
  Tenor   **979–83**
Domine non est.   a 6.   Sep., wanting Tenor   **979–83**
  Domine non est.   4-part opening of the same   **45**
  Sicut ablactatus.   a 4, from the same   **45**
Exaudiat te.   a 5.   Sep.   **984–8**
Justus es domine.   a 5   **984–8**
Lamentations.   a 5.   Sep.   **979–83, 984–8**
  Heth: peccatum peccavit.   Caph: O omnis populus.
  Teth: Sordes ejus.   Lamed: O vos omnes.
  Jod: Manum suam.   Mem: De excelso.
       Jerusalem convertere.
  O vos omnes.   a 4.   Fragment of the same   **45**
Lamentations.   a 6.   Sep., wanting Tenor   **979–83**
  Heth: peccatum peccavit.   Caph: O omnis populus.
  Teth: Sordes ejus.   Lamed: O vos omnes.
  Jod: Manum suam.   Mem: De excelso.
       Jerusalem convertere.
  Peccatum peccavit.   a 3.   Fragment of the same   **45**

WHYTE or WHITE (Robert)—*continued*.

Magnificat (fragments)   **45**
  Et sanctum nomen.   a 3.
  Quia fecit mihi.   a 4.
  Sicut erat in principio.   a 4.
  Sicut locutus.   a 4.
Manus tuae.   a 5.   Sep.   **979–83, 984–8**
 Fragments of same, Manus tuae, a 3; Veniant mihi, a 4   **45**
Miserere mei.   Pt. I. }
Cor mundum.   Pt. II. } a 5.   Sep.   **979–83, 984–8**
Porcio mea.   a 5.   Sep.   **979–83, 984–8**
Precamur sancte.   a 5.   Three settings   **979–83, 984–8**
  A fourth setting   **984–8**
Regina coeli.   a 5.   Sep., wanting Tenor   **979–83**
Tota pulchra.   a 6.   Sep., wanting Tenor   **979–83**

INSTRUMENTAL MUSIC.

In Nomine.   a 5.   **984–8**
Ut re me fa sol la.   For Organ   **371**

ANTHEMS, &c.

Lorde who shall dwell.   a 5.   *Burney*   **984–8**
O how glorious.   a 5.   *O. E. Ed.*   Organ parts   **88, 1001**
 The same adapted.   Let thy mercy full ears.   Sep.   A. T. B.
  only   **1220–4**
 The same adapted (probably by Aldrich).   I will wash.   Score
                 1205
O praise God in his holiness.   A.; T., 1 and 2; B., 1 and 2 **1220–4**
  Organ part   **1001**
O Lord deliver mee.   a 5 (for 2 Basses).   Sep., wanting Bass
                 56–60
The Lorde bless us.   a 5.   *O. E. Ed.*: *Barnard*.   **984–8**
  Organ   **1001**
 The same adapted.   ' O Lord rebuke me not ' (see *Husbands*).
  Scores   **11, 16**
  Organ part   **1230**
Three Phantasias a 5, of which the first is called ' Diapente '
  Sep.   **403–8, 473–8**
  In score   **2**
 The 1st.   Organ part   **67, 436**
  Sep.   **423–8**
 The 1st and 2nd.   Sep.   **716–20**
 The 1st and 2nd.   Organ part   **1004**
 The 2nd and 3rd.   Score   **44**

WHYTE or WHITE (William).
 Six Phantasies. a 6. Sep.   403–8, 473–8
   Score   2
  Of these the 1st, 2nd, 3rd, 4th, 5th. Sep. 423–8
  The 1st and 6th. Sep.   61–6
 Two Pavans. a 6. Sep.   423–8
  The second of these. Score   44

WICKENS (J.).
 6 Chants   1226

WILBYE (John). 1574–1638. See Fellowes, *The English Madrigal School*, vol. vi.
 Twelve Madrigals from the *Second Set of Madrigales*, 1609.
   Score, without words   33
  Ah cannot sighes. a 6.
  All pleasure. a 5.
  Downe in a valley. Pt. I. a 5.
  Hard destinies. Pt. II. a 5.
  Draw on sweet night. a 6.
  Long have I made. a 6.
  Oft have I vowde. a 5.
  Stay Coridon. a 6.
  Sweet hony sucking bees. Pt. I. a 5.
  Yet sweet take heed. Pt. II. a 5.
  Where most my thought. Pt. I. a 6.
  Dispightfull thus. Pt. II. a 6.
 Softly, oh softly drop mine eyes (1609), a 6. Score, without words 21
 Five Madrigals from the *Second Set of Madrigales*, 1609, with altered words. Sep.   1074–7
  At mercyes throane. a 3. (As fair as morn.)
  Flowe oh my teares. a 3. (Flourish ye hills.)
  How fadinge are the pleasures. a 3. (Ah cruel Amaryllis.)
  O what shall I doe. Pt. I. a 3. At thy feet I fall. Pt. II. a 3.
 Flora when I beholde. a 4. (Lady when I behold.) From the *First Set of English Madrigals*, 1598. Sep. 750–3

WILDER (Philip van). Called 'Mr. Philips of the king's privi-chamber' in 979–83. Lutenist to Henry VIII and Gentleman of the Privy Chamber to Edward VI. (See *Grove* under *Philips*.)
 Aspice Domine. a 5. Sep., wanting Tenor Book 979–83
 Pour vous aimer. Instrumental piece. a 5. Sep. 984–8
  (Both these are found in B. M. Add. MS. 31390.)

WILKINSON (Thomas). Early 17th century.
 Heare my prayer. V. A. a 5. Wanting Bass. Sep. 56–60
  Sep. A. T. B. only   1220–4
  Verse part only with Basso   49
 Preserve mee oh Lorde. V. A. a 5. Wanting Bass. Sep. 56–60
 Put mee not to rebuke. V. A. a 5. Wanting Bass. Sep. 56–60

WILLIAMS (   ). Of the end of the 17th century.
  Overture and 8 tunes for strings. Va. and Bass parts only.
        Sep.   **351–2**

WILSON (John). 1595–1674. Mus. Doc. Professor of Music in
  the University of Oxford.
  The whole contents of *Psalterium Carolinum*, 1657. Treble voice
    with Basso   **999**

Lord thou hast made.	O Lord thou seest.
Thou whose mercies.	Thou still the same.
Lord thou in heaven.	To thee my vprightness.
To thee I fly.	Of peace and reason Lord.
To thee my God.	With ready joy.
Our natiue freedome.	Lord thou who beauty.
Lord those whom thou.	Thou Lord who by thy wise.
Who vengeance.	Thou who all soules.
Through humane clouds.	Thou that alone art.
Oh my God to thee.	To thee my solitary prayers.
Eternall wisdom.	My God, my King (unfinished).
Thy mercy's Lord.	Lord thou sacred unity (words
My troubles, Lord.	only).
Lord I to thee direct.	Thou that fill'st heaven.

  Three Motets, a 3. Treble voice and Basso only. Score   **435**
      Exurgat Deus.
      Surge amica.
      Usque quo.

SONGS.

Beauty which all men admire. Treble Solo   **17**
Clora's false love. Treble voice part only   **365**
    (Printed in Playford's *Select Musicall Ayres and Dialogues*, 1652,
    and in Wilson's *Cheerfull Ayres*, 1660.)
Come constant harts. Treble Solo   **434**
    (A version printed in *Cheerfull Ayres*, 1660.)
Fairest Theina. Treble voice only   **438**
Greedy lover. Treble voice only   **438**
    (In *Cheerfull Ayres*, 1660.)
Not roses coucht. Treble Solo   **434**
    (A version in *Cheerfull Ayres*, 1660.)
O faire content. Treble Solo   **434**
Stay, lovely boy. Treble Solo   **49**
    (The Answer, *Black maid complain not*, may be by Wilson, but
    does not bear his name.)
Take o take those lips away. Treble Solo   **434**
    (Printed in Playford's *Select Musicall Ayres and Dialogues*, 1652.)
Though your sadnes. Treble Solo   **439**
    (Printed as *Though your strangeness* in *Cheerfull Ayres*, 1660.)
When Troy towne. Bass only   **366**
    (*Cheerfull Ayres*, 1660).

WINTERSALL (Robert). A 17th-century writer.

A number of pieces for the Virginal, of which those given below bear his name or initials. Probably many other pieces in this MS. are his.

> Coranto: Fantacy: 'Twitt twott Come fill the other pott': 'Ipswitch Loue': 'My loue is Lost': 'Now Found againe': 'So wage my Loue': 'Loue is a toy': 'All a morde' (i. e. Allemande): 'The Sarabrand to all a mord': 'The nimble mouse': 'High Landers march': A Sarabrand: 'The Mock': An Ayre: The Sarabrand to the Ayr: The Antick: An Ayre: A Sarabrand for Lute and Virginall: A Coranto: A Coranto for the Lute and Virginolls: The Sarabrand 'made for his Sweet Meetris susana pitts': The Sarabrand   **1175**

WISE (Michael). Child of the Chapel Royal under Capt. Cooke, 1660. Organist of Salisbury Cathedral; almoner and Master of the Children of St. Pauls. Killed by a blow 1687.

Awake put on thy strength. V. A. *Boyce*. Score	**12**
Organ part	**1226**
Awake up my glory. V. A. *Boyce*. Score	**12, 14**
Sep.	**623–6**
Organ part (twice)	**1234**
Behold how good. V. A. Counter Tenor only	**598**
Blessed is he. V. A. *Boyce*. Sep. Alto (V. and Chos.), T. and B. Chos. only	**1220–4**
Sep. Tr. 1 and 2. Verse and Chos. A. T. B. Chorus	**623–6**
I charge you O daughters. a 2 (Treble and Bass), from Playford's *Cantica Sacra*, 1674. Score	**18**
Open me the gates. V. A. Score	**12**
Organ part	**1233**
The Lord is my shepherd. V. A. Score	**12**
Thy beauty O Israel. V. A. *Boyce* (where it is said to have additions by Aldrich). Scores	**12, 16, 614**
Sep. 1 and 2 Tenor (V. and Chos.), B. (V. and Chos.)	**1220–4**
The wayes of Sion do mourn. V. A. Sep. T. (Verse and Chos.), A. and B. Chos. only	**1220–4**
Organ part	**1234**
Service in D mi.: Te D., Jub., Mag., N. Dim. Organ part	**1231**
Old Chiron thus preach't. a 2. (Treble and Bass)	**49**
(Printed in Playford's *Catch that catch can*, 1682, &c.)	
Poor Gally slaves. a 2. (Treble and Bass voice parts only.)	**350**

WITHY (Francis).
Single Chant. a 4. Score   48
A large number of examples of making closes, &c., in Francis
    Withy's copy of Simpson's *Compendium*, 1667, selected from
    various composers.   337

WITHY or WYTHIE (John).
Almaine. Bass only   1022
Phantazia. a 4, for 2 Basses   473–8
In nomine. a 5   473–8
Nineteen Fancies for 2 Basses and Organs, and one for Treble and
    Bass on a Ground   728–30
Instrumental piece in G mi., for Treble and Bass. By 'Mr.' Withy.
    Sep.   90–1

**WODSON (   ). Perhaps Thomas, Gentleman of the Chapel
    Royal, 1581.**
Miserere for Organ   371

WOODE (John). 'Batchelar of musicke.'
Exurge Domine. a 5, wanting Tenor   979–83

WOODSON (Leonard). Organist of Eton College. Died about 1643.
The mary gould of golden hew. Treble Solo   439

WOODCOCK (   ), probably Clement.
Two instrumental pieces. a 5. Sep.   984–8
        Browning.
        In nomine.

**WOODWARD (Dr.). 1744–77. Organist of Christ Church Cathedral,
    Dublin.**
Double Chant in B♭   1226

WYATT (   ).
Come shall wee three sing this Catch. Catch.   17

ZIANI (Pietro Andrea). Of Venice. Published from 1640 onwards.
Six Sonatas (a 5) for strings. Score   3
        In B♭ ma., G mi., E mi., F mi., A ma., F ma.
Sonata in D for strings and Trumpet with Organo. Score   771

APPENDIX

Christ Church Library, Oxford.
Music Manuscripts of which negative microfilms are held
31st March 1970

2	382–384	772–776
5	397–400	781
6	401–402	946–952
8	403–408	984–988
14	409–410	989–990
15	411–413	991
17	414–416	996
18	419–421	998
21	422	1001
23	423–428	1003
43	436	1004
44	437–438	1005
45	439	1006–1009
46	459–462	1016–1017
49	468–472	1018–1020
51	473–478	1022
53	517–520	1024
54	527–530	1025–1027
55	531–532	1034
56–60	598	1111
61–67	620	1124
75	621	1126
83	623–626	1128
87	628	1175
88	688	1176
89	691	1177
92	716–720	1178
350	725–727	1179
361	728–730	1183
362	732–735	1187
367–370	736–738	1210
371	754–759	1220–1224
377	765	1227
378	768–770	1230
379–381	771	1236